CHEAP AND EASY

Rose Elliot is one of Britain's most famous writers on vegetarian cookery. She is the author of many best-selling books and her original and imaginative style has made her a favourite among vegetarians and non-vegetarians alike. Her recipes range from creations of subtle sophistication to simple and cheap dishes for the novice cook and those on a tight budget.

Rose Elliot became a cookery writer by accident. She was planning to take a degree in history when she met and married her husband and became involved in cookery, entertaining and bringing up a family. For many years she has tried out all her recipes at home, the very best of which she has included in her books.

ROSE ELLIOT

Cheap and Easy

Fast, flavoursome and inexpensive
dishes from Britain's best-known writer
on vegetarian cookery

Fontana/Collins

First published in Fontana Paperbacks 1988

© Rose Elliot 1988

Illustrations by Vana Haggerty

Made and printed in Great Britain by
William Collins Sons & Co. Ltd, Glasgow

CONTENTS

To my student daughters,
Katy and Margaret,
with all love

Introduction

Cheap Food, Good Food

There's something very satisfying about producing a tasty, nourishing meal at a rock bottom price – and not having to spend hours in the kitchen in order to do it!

Cheap food can undoubtedly be good food, tasty, healthy and quick to make.

There are in the world a wealth of colourful and delicious dishes which have sustained our forebears for generations and still do so today. These use basic, cheap foods which do not need elaborate refining or packaging. They are additive-free, full of fibre and packed with nutrients — and they taste great!

Along with these basic international recipes are favourites from a new and rapidly developing culinary art, vegetarian cookery. These, too, use the basic, unprocessed foods and bring further variety and interest to money-saving meals.

Including some of these dishes in your weekly menus can save pounds; basing your week's menus entirely on them can cut your expenses by at least a third.

Feeling Good, Looking Great

Contrary to what people think, cheap meals can actually be better for you in terms of health and nutrition, than richer, more expensive meals. It's well known that during the last war people in Britain were healthier on the meagre diet which rationing enforced.

This is because such a diet relies on basic foods such as potatoes, pasta, wholemeal bread, grains and pulses. All these contain fibre, are rich in nutrients and free from additives. If you base your meals on these staples, include small quantities of eggs and dairy produce, have a good source of vitamin C each day and, if possible, a good serving of green vegetables, you will be well-nourished, look fit and feel good. Good sources of vitamin C are oranges or grapefruit, or some orange or grapefruit juice, a good salad, or a good serving of ·potatoes, a large piece of melon or a bowl of strawberries.

If you're overweight, you'll probably find that you shed the extra pounds naturally, as long as you keep away from the puddings, pies and cakes, which provide extra fillers for families and very active people. Replace ordinary milk with skim milk and use reduced fat cheese for useful savings in calories.

Saving Time, Saving Money

It's possible to save a great deal of time and money by following a few simple guidelines:

USE FOOD IN SEASON

Buying fresh food in season makes sound economic sense, as well as ensuring that you get the best quality. If you grow your own produce and can freeze some of it, that saves even more money. Making use of some of the free wild food to be found, such as chestnuts, blackberries, bilberries, sea spinach and mushrooms can be an extra occasional bonus, too, though probably not enough to make much difference to the weekly budget.

MAKE FULL USE OF VEGETABLES

Vegetables represent excellent value for money; they're full of nourishment, and, being high in fibre, they're filling and health-giving. Make them the basis of meals often: there are plenty of main-meal vegetable recipes in this book. Serve a vegetable or salad alongside a main course for extra interest and to make the more expensive ingredients go further.

USE THE BASIC PROTEINS

These are the grains, lentils, beans and pasta which have sustained generations the world over. Again, these are excellent value, both in terms of health and money. Add just small quantities of more concentrated proteins such as eggs, cheese and nuts to turn them into tasty and highly nutritious meals.

PLAN AHEAD

This does not necessarily mean you have to plan out meals for a whole week, but it helps to think in terms of two or three days at a time, because it doesn't take any time to cook an extra amount of rice or lentils, and very little time to fry an extra onion, prepare a double quantity of potatoes, breadcrumbs or grated cheese or make some extra mashed potatoes, and these can really save time and effort in the future.

Here are some examples of menus which 'think ahead'; you don't have to serve the second meal on the following day if you have a fridge as left-overs will keep for at least a day, if not two or three, covered and refrigerated:

Lentil roast or *pease pudding* or *carrot and hazelnut roast* – make enough to serve this once hot with roast potatoes, gravy and a cooked vegetable, and once cold in slices, with a chutney or a yogurt and chopped herb dressing and some salad or hot boiled brown rice – (and make extra of that, while you're about it, too – see below!). When you're par-boiling the potatoes to roast them, do a double quantity and save some to make into a *potato hotpot* or *potato and mushroom gratin* – and while you're making the sauce for these, make a double quantity so you can quickly rustle up *easy mushrooms baked in a cheese sauce* to serve with crusty bread another day!

Tomatoes stuffed with sweetcorn, served on brown rice – make a double quantity of rice and use the second batch for *left-over rice dish*; likewise, if you're serving delicious ratatouille with some brown rice, do extra rice and make the second batch into a rice salad, for serving with crusty rolls and watercress another day.

Cheese and courgette gratin – again, cook a double batch of brown rice, and use the second batch for *rice croquettes*.

When you're making mashed potatoes to serve with a meal, make a double quantity ready for topping a *lentil shepherd's pie* or *quick red bean and tomato bake*, or for making into *nutty potato cakes* as a quick meal to serve with a green salad, or perhaps a Greek salad, for added interest.

If you're making pastry, perhaps for a *wholewheat cheese and onion pie* or *potato and mushroom pasties* (which make a good lunchbox item), prepare extra and make a flan case, then you can quickly whizz up a *mixed vegetable flan* or a *sweetcorn soufflé flan* another day. If you make a bit extra on top of that, you can bake some *jam tarts*, which are a healthy treat for children when made with wholewheat pastry and a reduced-sugar jam.

A basic semolina mix, page 171, can be used to make *cheese fritters* and *Italian gnocchi*, both of which are perennial favourites. The cheese fritters are good served with parsley sauce, chips or new potatoes and a cooked vegetable; the gnocchi is nice with a tomato and onion salad.

Some recipes, which you like and never get tired of, are worth making in a double amount, so that you can have two servings of them in the week. *Cheese fritters* come into that category in my family, and I also very much like the hearty soup, *Pistou*, with its Provençal flavouring. *Hummus* is also very addictive, once you get the taste for it, served with lots of warm wholewheat pitta bread and perhaps some sticks of carrot, raw celery and green or red pepper. *Ratatouille*, which I've already mentioned, is a dish which I, personally, never get tired of, and a double batch of this is useful, as you can serve it once with hot cooked brown rice, perhaps with some fresh chopped herbs forked through the rice, and then you can have the rest cold, as a salad, on another day, or you can use it to fill a baked flan case or pancakes. You can also put the ratatouille into a shallow ovenproof dish, make some hollows in it and break an egg into each hollow, then bake in a moderate oven until the eggs are just set, and serve with crusty bread.

It's always useful to make more wholemeal breadcrumbs than you need, especially if you've got a food processor to make them and a freezer in which to store them. I keep breadcrumbs in a polythene bag in the freezer, ready for instant use, and whizz up left-over slices of bread and the ends of loaves to add to them. Then they're ready for dishes such as *stuffed cabbage rolls, marrow with sage and onion stuffing, tomato bread pudding* or *mushroom and tomato layer.*

Some dishes, such as *stuffed jacket potatoes, Yorkshire pudding, pasta rings with leeks and cheese, quick pizza, felafel in pitta pockets, potato and cheese layer, steamed vegetable pudding, macaroni bake* or *macaroni cheese*, are useful 'one-off' dishes, though you could cook enough macaroni for both the bake and macaroni cheese while you're about it. If you also make extra cheese sauce when you're making the macaroni cheese, you'd be able to make *cauliflower, Stilton and walnut bake* very quickly the next day.

In fact, half an hour spent with this recipe book and a notepad and pencil, working out some inter-related meals like this, which appeal to you, and making a shopping list, could save you several hours of time during the week.

One more time-saver and flavour-enhancer: I've found fresh chopped parsley to be invaluable in adding flavour to dishes made from cheap ingredients. It really is worth the expense – or, better still, worth the effort of growing some (lots). Then wash and chop it by the handful so that you have a polythene bag of it in the freezer, ready for instant use.

Keep the Basics in the Storecupboard

If you always keep a few staples in the storecupboard, you'll be able to rustle up a quick meal in next to no time. For instance with these staples to hand, you could make any of the dishes which follow:

plain wholewheat flour	*potatoes*
brazil nuts	*carrots*
green lentils, split red lentils	*onions*
wholemeal bread	*garlic*
canned tomatoes	*olive oil*
pasta	*butter*
rolled oats	*eggs*
dried thyme, basil or oregano	*cheese*
lemon juice	*milk and plain yogurt*

Savoury brazil nut fritters with a yogurt and chopped onion sauce (or chutney); *golden lentil soup* with warm wholewheat bread; *potato and onion soup* with *toasted cheese sandwiches; quick French onion soup; pasta with grated cheese; potato and onion fry; even easier potato cakes; potato pizza; macaroni cheese, cheesy potato layer, lentil roast* and, if you've got some mustard (or leave it out), *savoury bread and butter pudding.* And if you add to these basics a couple of courgettes, a couple of green peppers, some celery and some curry powder, you could also make *Spanish omelette, green lentil soup* and *lentils with tomatoes and thyme* for serving with crusty bread. And with some fresh ginger and parsley in your fridge and a bottle of chilli powder on the shelf, you could add to this list *spicy lentil burgers* and probably quite a few other quick and easy recipes in this book, too.

Give Yourself Some Treats

Lentil roast and cabbage, or *pasta and grated cheese* may be great, healthy, money-saving food, but you need something a bit more luxurious every so often to keep your inspiration up! So plan for some special dishes sometimes. These may be a little more expensive or a little more trouble to make, but they're a nice change and a pleasant tonic. Dishes such as *cheese fondue* served with lots of crusty French bread and some dry white wine; *deep fried Camembert* with some brown rice and apricot or mango chutney; a *real yeast pizza* which is fun to make and very satisfying, or *couscous with spicy vegetable stew,* delicious and fragrantly flavoured. Other dishes which are a bit special are *stuffed avocado* which is nice served on a base of creamy, light mashed potato with a crunchy side salad; *stuffed aubergines* which are good with saute or new potatoes and a cooked vegetable such as French beans; *individual cheese soufflés* served with salad with a really good dressing; *cheese and aubergine bake* or *Middle Eastern chick pea stew* which are both good with crusty bread and some red wine; *spinach roulade with mushroom filling* with some lightly-cooked carrots and French beans or courgettes; *cauliflower and green pea terrine* with crusty bread, tomato and onion salad and some wine;

creamy pasta with a green salad. *Mushroom-stuffed pancakes* can also be delicious as can *vegetable rice with roasted nuts* (especially if you splash out and buy some whole roasted cashew nuts!) and *carrot and fresh ginger soup* (especially if you include the optional cream) or *Greek salad* as first courses.

Alternatively, if you have a sweet tooth, you may feel more like turning to the puddings and cakes sections of this book with *strawberry tart, steamed pudding, rhubarb crumble, old fashioned fruit cake, gingerbread or jam sandwich cake* as special treats.

Pots and Pans

To make all these dishes, having the right equipment can save hours of time, as well as energy. However, cheap and easy cooking does not demand lots of complicated gadgets. A food processor does save time and effort, but is only essential for one or two of the recipes in this book. The rest rely on the minumum of simple equipment. Microwaving instructions are included at the end of the book, not because it is in any way essential to have a microwave, but because many people have told me that they would find them useful: the same applies to the deep freeze, although I do think this is a time-saving piece of equipment to have, especially if you're cooking for just one or two people. But the necessary equipment is as follows:

A good sharp knife The traditional Sabatier ones are expensive but last well and once you've used one, you won't want to use anything else. Choose a steel or stainless steel one with a 13cm/5 inch blade and make sure it is the real thing, with the blade riveted into the handle. You'll need a steel to sharpen it on too.

A sturdy wooden chopping board A good size is 2cm (1 inch) thick and not less than 40 × 30cm (16 × 12 inches). This will double as a board for rolling out pastry on, too.

Clear glass bowls in several sizes

Several casserole dishes

A colander Preferably a stainless steel one, which will last for ever and can double as a steamer.

13

An egg whisk   A metal balloon type is quite cheap to buy.

A frying pan   Ideally it's useful to have two, one measuring 27.5cm (10¾ inches) across, for general frying and one measuring 20cm (8 inches) for pancakes.

A rolling pin   A plain wooden one without handles is best.

A box grater   which you can stand on your chopping board and which has different sizes of holes.

A measuring jug

A palette knife and a fish slice

Several wooden spoons of different sizes

A potato peeler

A large metal sieve and a large nylon sieve

A large, medium and small saucepan   My preference is for stainless steel or good quality enamel.

A pressure cooker   Not essential, but useful for preparing beans and lentils quickly and for making soups. If you're buying a new one, choose a stainless steel one.

Kitchen scales   are useful, but the recipes in this book have been planned so that these are not essential.

In addition to these basics, you'll need some old tablespoons, forks and teaspoons for cooking jobs; also various baking tins, a baking tray and wire cooling rack.

Stocking the Shelves

BASIC STAPLES Dried and canned beans, lentils, pasta, wholemeal flours, rice and other grains. Buy in fairly small quantities from a shop with a rapid turnover to ensure freshness. The same applies to nuts.

Dairy Produce: Free range eggs, milk, yogurt – which you can make cheaply at home (see page 192) – small amounts of cream and soured cream for occasional use. A basic Cheddar-type cheese for cooking (I use a vegetarian Cheddar), and the occasional use of other cheeses such as Mozzarella, Camembert, Parmesan and soft white cheeses to add interest to meals.

Fats: Worth spending money on from the health point of view. My preference is for a good quality unsalted butter on the table and for baking; virgin olive oil for salad dressings and dishes where the flavour is important, and ground nut oil (or olive oil) for frying, because these oils are more stable at high temperatures and so healthier. Watch and cut back on the amount of fat you use, both to save money, and make your food healthier.

Sweetenings: Choose real unrefined sugars where possible; dark molasses sugar for dishes which can take the flavour; lighter brown sugars or real demerara sugar for more delicate flavours. A jar of vanilla sugar is useful to have for occasional use in delicate dishes; to make this, break a vanilla pod in half and bury the halves in a jar of castor sugar. Clear honey, golden syrup and black treacle are handy for occasional use, as is jam: homemade, or one of the reduced sugar or no-added sugar jams.

Flavourings: Sea salt and black pepper which you will mill yourself in a pepper grinder make all the difference to the flavour of dishes. Dry mustard is another useful flavouring, as are soy sauce – choose a natural one, without preservatives and colouring – yeast extract, lemon juice and tabasco. Parsley is very useful, as I've already mentioned. Good vegetarian stock powders are available and are useful for soups. Fresh basil is another extremely useful flavouring, as is fresh mint. Other useful herbs and spices, worth collecting gradually, are cardamom, cinnamon – ground, and stick – ginger, bay leaves, chilli powder, cloves, ground coriander, ground and whole cumin seeds, caraway seeds, dill weed, fennel seeds, turmeric, rosemary, thyme, mace, oregano, mixed herbs, curry powder, paprika, ground ginger. Garlic salt and celery salt are useful for quick use. Fresh garlic and fresh ginger are also very useful flavourings. Vanilla pod and real vanilla essence are useful, so is nutmeg – buy it whole and grate on the fine edge of a box grater or with a special little nutmeg grater.
Wine vinegar is essential for making good salad dressings – I like the red wine vinegar best – and it's useful to have a jar of good quality mayonnaise, such as Hellman's, in the fridge.

1 Super Soups

Soups are wonderful time and money-savers. They can be made extremely quickly and cheaply, and if you serve a soup at the beginning of the meal, not only is it warming and welcoming, it also means that the main course can be that much lighter. If you choose one of the 'big soups' such as pistou, lentil or leek and potato, it can be a main course in itself, so you don't have to bother with separate vegetables or any accompaniments, except perhaps for some warm bread rolls or, if you feel like preparing them, some dumplings or hot garlic or herb bread.

TO MAKE DUMPLINGS

Put 6 heaped tablespoons of wholemeal flour into a bowl with 1½ teaspoons baking powder, ½ teaspoon salt and 65 g (2½ oz) grated hard butter and mix together. Then add 1 teaspoonful of yeast extract dissolved in a couple of tablespoons of water and mix; add more water, to make a soft dough. Then form into eight even-sized balls. Drop the dumplings into half a panful of gently simmering water, and simmer them for 20 minutes, until puffed up. Drain them and serve with soup.

TO MAKE GARLIC OR HERB BREAD

Blend a crushed garlic clove or 2 teaspoonfuls of chopped fresh herbs such as chives, thyme and marjoram (or the frozen chopped mixed herbs you can buy) into 50 g (2 oz) soft butter. Take half a French stick – white or brown – and cut it, as if you were going to slice it, but don't go right through the base. Butter the pieces generously on both sides, pulling them open to do so, then press them all together again, wrap the loaf in foil and heat through in a hot oven – 200°C/400°F/Gas Mark 6 – for 15–20 minutes, or wrapped in greaseproof paper, in a microwave on full power for 5 minutes, until the butter has melted and the crust is crisp. Serve at once. For a 1-person quantity, just mix a little butter with garlic, as described, and spread it on both sides of slices of bread. Heat the bread under the grill until the butter has melted and the bread is slightly crisp on one side, then turn the bread over and do the other side.

QUANTITIES

Most of the soups which follow will serve four people. They can easily be halved if you just want to make enough for one or two, and any that's over will keep for 2–3 days covered with clingfilm in the fridge. If you're only cooking for one person, it can be a great time-saver to make up the full 4-person quantity of soup while you're about it and freeze what you don't need in 1-person portions for the future.

FREEZING AND REHEATING

All the soups will freeze; just put them into a suitable container and freeze them when they are cold. If you're short of containers, line a bowl or jug with a polythene bag or layer of foil, pour the soup in, then freeze, and remove the bowl or jug when the soup is frozen. Secure the bag or arrange the foil so that the soup is completely covered; label.

When you want to use the soup, it's best to let it thaw out completely, which can take several hours, depending on the quantity, so remember to get the soup out of the freezer in good time. Then reheat the soup gently either in a saucepan on top of the stove, or in a bowl in a microwave. In the microwave it can take about 10 minutes, and it's helpful to give the mixture a stir once or twice, as the soup at the sides of the bowl gets hot before the soup in the centre.

Carrot and Ginger Soup

This soup has a delicate flavour, smooth texture and beautiful colour which make it suitable for serving as a first course for a special meal, yet it can be made for very little cost. Simply quarter or halve the ingredients if you're making it for one or two people, or double up for six or eight.

Serves 4   100 calories in each serving

1 onion, peeled and chopped
15 g (½ oz) butter
1 medium-sized potato, peeled
   and cubed
450 g (1 lb) carrots, scraped and
   sliced

1 teaspoon grated fresh ginger
800 ml (1½ pints) water
4 tablespoons cream, optional
salt and freshly ground black
   pepper

Fry the onion gently in the butter in a large saucepan for 5 minutes, then add the potato, carrots, ginger and a sprinkling of salt and fry for a further 10 minutes, with a lid on the pan, stirring from time to time. Add the water, bring up to the boil, then simmer gently for about 15 minutes, until the vegetables are cooked. Sieve, or liquidize then sieve, the mixture. Return to the rinsed-out saucepan, season with salt and pepper. Top each bowlful with a spoonful of cream, if you're using this.

Green Lentil Soup

This soup re-heats well. Some hot garlic bread goes well with it. These quantities can be quartered or halved for one or two people and the cooking time remains the same.

Serves 4   240 calories in each serving

1 onion, peeled and chopped
1 stick of celery, chopped
1 carrot, scraped and diced
1 green pepper, de-seeded and
  chopped
1 medium-sized potato, peeled
  and diced
1 garlic clove, crushed

½ teaspoon curry powder
½ teaspoon basil
225 g (8 oz) green lentils
2½ pints vegetable stock or
  water
425 g (15 oz) can tomatoes
salt and freshly ground black
  pepper

Put all the ingredients into a large saucepan, bring to the boil, then simmer gently for about 40 minutes, until the lentils are tender. Season with salt and pepper.

Golden Lentil Soup

Quite different from the last soup, this one is made from the split orange lentils and is a satisfying, comforting soup. It makes an excellent cheap filling main course with crusty wholemeal rolls or garlic bread. If you've got a pressure-cooker, you can make it in about 10 minutes; even without, it can be made from start to finish in half an hour. Use a quarter or half these ingredients, and the same cooking time, for one or two people.

Serves 4   200 calories in each serving

1 large onion, chopped
15 g (½ oz) butter
225 g (8 oz) split red lentils
1 litre (1¾ pints) water or
   vegetable stock

1–2 teaspoons lemon juice
salt and freshly ground black
   pepper

Fry the onion in the butter in a saucepan or pressure-cooker pan, for 10 minutes, until tender but not browned. Add the lentils and stir for 1–2 minutes, then put in the stock or water. Bring to the boil, then half cover the pan and leave the soup to simmer gently for 20 minutes, until the lentils are very tender and pale-coloured. Or cook in a pressure-cooker for 5 minutes. Beat the soup with a spoon to break up the lentils and make it smoother, or liquidize. Add the lemon juice and salt and pepper to taste.

Potato and Leek Soup

This makes a thick, chunky soup, a real meal in itself on a cold day. For a lighter result, liquidize the soup and add enough extra water to make it the consistency you want. For real luxury, add a spoonful or two of cream and top with some chopped chives. Halve these quantities for one or two servings.

Serves 3–4   310–410 calories in each serving

25 g (1 oz) butter
3 medium-sized leeks, washed
   and sliced
3 large potatoes, peeled and
   diced

3 teaspoons vegetable broth
   powder (page 15)
1 litre (1¾ pints) water
salt and freshly ground black
   pepper

Melt the butter in a large saucepan, then add the leeks and potatoes and fry these very gently, with a lid on the pan, for 10 minutes, stirring often. Sprinkle the broth powder and a little salt and pepper over the potatoes and leeks, stir, then continue to cook gently, still covered, for a further 10 minutes, stirring often. It doesn't matter if the vegetables brown slightly, but don't let them get too brown. Add the water, stir, then simmer for 5–10 minutes, until the vegetables are cooked. Check seasoning, then serve.

Potato and Onion Soup

This is an excellent variation. Replace the leeks with 2 large onions; peel, chop and fry with the potatoes.

Lettuce Soup

This is a soup which can be made for very little cost if you use the outer leaves of lettuce which you would otherwise throw away, or overgrown (or very cheap) lettuce when there's a glut. It's also good made with other green leaves such as spinach, sea kale and sorrel. It's quite filling, and with some wholemeal bread makes a good lunch. For special occasions it's extra good with some single cream swirled on top of each bowlful. You need a liquidizer for this one. Use a quarter of these quantities for one person, half for two, and the same cooking time.

Makes 4 good bowlfuls   300 calories in each serving

1 onion, peeled and chopped
3 large potatoes, peeled and cut
   into even sized pieces
25 g (1 oz) butter
450 g (1 lb) outer lettuce leaves,
   washed and roughly chopped

800 ml (1½ pints) water
salt and freshly ground black
   pepper

22

Fry the onion and potatoes in the butter in a large saucepan for 10 minutes until beginning to soften but not browned. Add the lettuce and cook for a further 2–3 minutes, then add the water. Bring up to the boil, then simmer for 15–20 minutes, until the potatoes are tender. Liquidize, return the soup to the rinsed-out saucepan, season, re-heat and serve.

French Onion Soup

This soup is very filling, and makes a good main course, followed by fruit or a light pudding. Halve these ingredients for one serving.

Makes 2 large bowlfuls   330 calories in each serving

4 large onions, peeled and thinly
   sliced
15 g (½ oz) butter
salt, sugar and freshly ground
   black pepper
800 ml (1½) pints stock

1 garlic clove, crushed
few drops lemon juice
salt and freshly ground black
   pepper
2 slices French bread
50 g (2 oz) grated cheese

Melt the butter in a large saucepan and fry the onions for 10 minutes until they're soft. Season with salt, pepper and a little sugar (about 2 teaspoons), then continue to fry for a further 10–15 minutes, until the onions are golden brown. Don't let them burn. Then add the stock, garlic, and a few drops of lemon juice. Bring the soup to the boil and let it simmer for about 10 minutes, then check seasoning. To serve the soup put a piece of bread into each soup bowl, pour the soup in on top, sprinkle with grated cheese, and grill until golden brown and melted. Serve immediately.

Pistou

This easy-to make, tasty and very filling bean soup from southern France makes a complete main course. If you're using dried beans, you need to soak and cook them beforehand. This soup reheats well. Make half these quantities for one or two people, and cook for the same amount of time.

Serves 4   300 calories in each serving

1 onion, peeled and chopped
2 tablespoons oil (preferably
   olive oil)
125 g (4 oz) haricot beans,
   soaked and cooked, or 425 g
   (15 oz) can cannellini beans
2 carrots, diced
2 potatoes, peeled and diced
3 leeks or courgettes, washed
   and sliced

425 g (15 oz) can tomatoes
2 garlic cloves, crushed
1 teaspoon dried basil or 1–2
   tablespoons chopped fresh
   basil
1 litre (1¾) pints water or
   stock
50 g (2 oz) thin pasta or pasta
   shapes
salt and freshly ground black
   pepper

Fry the onion in the oil for 5 minutes, then add the drained beans, all the vegetables, garlic, some seasoning, and the basil if you're using dried, and cook for a further 5 minutes. Then add the stock, and simmer for 20–30 minutes. After that, add the pasta and cook for a further 10 minutes. If you're using fresh basil, add this now; season to taste with salt and pepper.

Root Vegetable Soup

This is a tasty and economical winter soup. Serve it with warm wholemeal rolls or with some grated cheese sprinkled over the top if you want to make it into more of a meal. Use a quarter or half of these quantities for one or two people, cooking for the same length of time.

Serves 4   150 calories in each serving

1.2l (2 pints) water
2 large carrots, scraped and
    sliced
2 onions, peeled and sliced
2 medium-sized potatoes,
    peeled and diced

1 small swede (about 225 g (8
    oz)) peeled and diced
1 turnip (about 225 g (8 oz))
    peeled and diced
4 sticks of celery, chopped
15 g (½ oz) butter

Put the water into a large saucepan, add all the vegetables and bring to the boil. Simmer gently, with a lid on the saucepan, until all the vegetables are tender – about 30 minutes. Add the butter and mash some of the vegetables a bit, to thicken the soup, or liquidize a cupful of the soup, then add to the remainder.

2 Saucy Suppers

A bechamel or cheese sauce is quick to make and can turn a few vegetables, some hard-boiled eggs or left-over cooked rice into a tasty meal. It's always useful to have some sauce in the fridge or the freezer, so it's worth making up more than you need. It will keep well in the fridge for 2–3 days, or for several weeks in the freezer.

FREEZING AND REHEATING

Freeze the sauce in the portion-size that you usually need. Clean yogurt or cottage cheese cartons make convenient containers, or you can use a polythene bag – open the bag and put it inside a jug to make it easier to fill.

To reheat, let the sauce thaw out for an hour or so, then reheat it gently in a saucepan on top of the stove, or in a non-metal bowl in a microwave, for about 5 minutes, stirring it several times.

Basic Béchamel Sauce

This white sauce is the basis of cheese sauce, parsley sauce and mushroom sauce too. This recipe makes enough for four people, but the quantities can easily be halved. For one person, it may be worth making a ½ pint quantity and freezing or keeping half, but if you only want enough for one, use 15 g (½ oz) butter, 1 level tablespoonful of flour and 150 ml (¼ pint) milk.

Makes 600 ml (1 pint)   Total calories about 1,020

600 ml (1 pint) milk
small piece of peeled onion,
*   small scraped carrot*
a bay leaf, 6 peppercorns and a
*   few fresh parsley stalks if*
*   available*

50 g (2 oz) butter or margarine
2 rounded tablespoons flour

Put the milk with the onion, scraped carrot, bay leaf, peppercorns and parsley stalks, if you have them. Bring to the boil, then cover and leave to stand for 15 minutes. Then strain, reserving the milk. Melt the butter in a medium-sized saucepan and stir in the flour. Cook for a moment or two, then add the reserved milk. Stir over the heat until thickened. It will be lumpy at first, but as you continue to stir and cook the lumps will disappear. If there are any obstinate ones, however, whisking the sauce will get rid of them. If you are planning to add the sauce to a dish which will have further cooking, you can add the seasoning and use the sauce as soon as it is thickened. If the sauce won't have further cooking, leave it to simmer over a low heat for 10 minutes, to cook the flour.

Parsley Sauce

For parsley sauce, add a couple of heaped tablespoons of chopped parsley to the basic béchamel sauce.

Mushroom Sauce

Add 125 g (4 oz) finely chopped button mushrooms to the basic béchamel sauce once it has thickened.

Basic Cheese Sauce

Makes 600 ml (1 pint) serves 4   Total calories 1,260–1,500

600 ml (1 pint) béchamel sauce   salt and freshly ground black
50–100 g (2–4 oz) grated cheese   pepper
1 teaspoon made mustard

If you are going to use the cheese sauce for a dish which will then have further cooking (such as macaroni cheese), add the grated cheese, mustard and seasoning to the sauce as soon as it has thickened and you have taken it off the heat. If you are going to use the sauce without further cooking – poured over cooked vegetables, for instance – let it simmer for 10–15 minutes after thickening, to cook the flour, then remove from the heat and add the cheese, mustard and seasonings.

Tomato Sauce

Tomato sauce is easy to make and, like cheese sauce and béchamel sauce, can be poured over cooked vegetables, sprinkled with crumbs and grated cheese, and baked, to make a tasty main course.

It's also useful for serving with croquettes and other savoury dishes where some moisture and a dash of colour would make the meal more delicious and appetizing.

Makes about 300 ml (½ pint) Serves 2   Total calories about 200

1 onion, peeled and chopped
1 tablespoon oil
1 garlic clove, crushed

425 g (15 oz) can tomatoes, chopped
salt and freshly ground black pepper

Fry the onion in the oil for 10 minutes, until tender but not browned. Then add the garlic and tomatoes and cook for 2–3 minutes, until heated through. Season with salt and pepper. This sauce can be used as it is, or liquidized for a smoother texture.

Vegetarian Gravy

Makes about 300 ml (½ pint) Serves 2–3   total calories about 180

1 onion, peeled and chopped
1 tablespoon oil
1 tablespoon flour
1 garlic clove, crushed
300 ml (½ pint) water

2–3 tablespoons soy sauce
1 teaspoon yeast extract
salt and freshly ground black pepper

Fry the onion in the oil for 10 minutes, allowing it to brown a bit, then add the flour and cook until nut-brown in colour, then stir in the garlic, 300 ml (½ pint) water or water strained from cooked vegetables. Simmer for 5–10 minutes, to cook the flour, then add the soy sauce (which darkens as well as flavours the gravy), yeast extract and salt and pepper to taste.

Vegetables in Cheese Sauce

This is very quick and easy, especially if you've got some sauce ready-made in the freezer. For best results, choose vegetables which cook in the same amount of time, or stick to one type. Mixed root vegetables are good, perhaps with some sliced leek or onion added; or marrow or courgettes in the summer. A packet of frozen mixed vegetables gives even speedier results. These quantities can be halved or quartered for two people or a single serving.

Serves 4   490 calories in each serving

900 g (2 lb) mixed vegetables   *4 tablespoons grated cheese*
600 ml (1 pint) cheese sauce
4 heaped tablespoons fresh or
  dried breadcrumbs

Cook the vegetables in a little fast-boiling, lightly-salted water until they're just tender, then drain them well. Prepare a hot grill. Add the sauce to the vegetables, check the seasoning. Pour the mixture into a large shallow ovenproof dish which will fit under the grill. Sprinkle the breadcrumbs and cheese over the top. Grill until the top is golden brown and crunchy and the inside hot and bubbling.

Cauliflower, Stilton and Walnut Bake

Strongly-flavoured cheeses can work out quite cheap because you only need a little. This recipe works equally well if you halve or quarter the quantities, using a small cauliflower (or half).

Serves 4   640 calories in each serving

1 large cauliflower, broken into
    florets
50 g (2 oz) walnut pieces,
    coarsely chopped
50–75 g (2–3 oz) Stilton cheese,
    grated
600 ml (1 pint) cheese sauce

4 heaped tablespoons
    wholewheat breadcrumbs
4 tablespoons grated Cheddar-
    type cheese
salt and freshly ground black
    pepper

Cook the cauliflower in ½ inch of boiling water for 4–5 minutes, then drain. Put the cauliflower in the base of a lightly-greased shallow ovenproof dish, sprinkle with the chopped walnuts. Set the oven to 200°C/400°F/Gas Mark 6 or prepare a moderate grill. Add the Stilton to the cheese sauce, then pour evenly over the cauliflower. Sprinkle the crumbs and grated cheese over the top. Bake for 20–30 minutes, or put under the grill for about 10 minutes, until the top is crispy and the inside hot and bubbly. Some watercress goes well with this, or sliced firm tomatoes, and either potatoes baked in their jackets or crusty rolls.

Easy Mushrooms Baked in Cheese Sauce

Very fast to make, and a wonderful way of serving those big open mushrooms. This recipe can easily be doubled for four people, or halved for one. Serve with hot wholewheat toast or some cooked rice.

Serves 2   330 calories in each serving

6–8 large open mushrooms
salt and freshly ground black
    pepper

300 ml (½ pint) cheese sauce

Set the oven to 200°C/400°F/Gas Mark 6. Wash the mushrooms, then put them black-side up in a single layer in a lightly-greased shallow ovenproof dish. Sprinkle with salt and pepper, then spoon the sauce evenly over all the mushrooms. Bake for about 30 minutes, until the mushrooms are tender when pierced with a sharp knife and the sauce is browned on top and bubbling.

3 Bread Winners

Bread is wonderful as the basis of cheap, filling, and speedy meals. As well as the bread-based dishes in this chapter, breadcrumbs feature in a number of recipes in other sections of this book.

Wholemeal breadcrumbs are both tasty and good for you. You can buy wholemeal breadcrumbs at health shops (and probably at some supermarkets, the rate at which the wholemeal trend is catching on). They are also very easy to make at home, especially if you have a food processor or blender. To make crumbs, you need bread which is a day or two old. Cut off the crusts and crumble the bread between your fingers, or pop chunks of bread into a food processor or blender and whizz for a moment or two. If you have a freezer, it's worth making any left-over pieces of bread into crumbs and putting them into a polythene bag in the freezer. They can be used straight from the freezer.

Alternatively, you can dry out slices of bread in the bottom of the oven while something else is cooking, or in a microwave (they only take 5 minutes or so). Then crush them with a rolling pin. It's useful to have both fresh and dried breadcrumbs available.

BREADCRUMB-BASED DISHES

Mushroom and Tomato Layer

A savoury and delicious mixture; serve with a cooked vegetable, such as cauliflower. This works satisfactorily in a smaller quantity; halve or quarter the amounts to make enough for a double or single serving and bake for about 15 minutes only.

Serves 4   450 calories in each serving

50 g (2 oz) butter
1 onion, peeled and finely
   chopped
12 heaped tablespoons soft
   wholewheat breadcrumbs
100 g (4 oz) chopped nuts
1 teaspoon mixed herbs

225 g (8 oz) mushrooms,
   washed and chopped
450 g (1 lb) tomatoes, skinned
   and chopped, or a 425 g (15
   oz) can, drained
salt and freshly ground black
   pepper

Melt the butter and fry the onion and breadcrumbs for about 10 minutes, until they're crisp. Remove from the heat and stir in the nuts, herbs and seasoning to taste. Set the oven to 200°C/400°F/Gas Mark 6. Mix together the mushrooms and tomatoes; season with salt and pepper. Put a layer of the crumb mixture into an ovenproof dish and cover with half the mushroom mixture. Continue in layers, ending with the crumb mixture. Bake for 30 minutes.

Parsley Burgers

Very cheap and surprisingly good. A variation is to add some chopped black olives.

Serves 1   240 calories in each serving

2 eggs, beaten
6 heaped tablespoons soft
  wholewheat breadcrumbs
1 small onion, peeled and finely
  chopped

4 tablespoons chopped fresh
  parsley
salt and freshly ground black
  pepper
oil for shallow-frying

Add the breadcrumbs, onion and parsley to the beaten egg and season to taste. Pour enough oil into a frying pan to cover the base thinly and heat. Form the parsley mixture into burgers and fry in the oil for about 3 minutes on both sides, until crisp. Drain on kitchen paper. Serve with salad.

SLICES OF BREAD BASE

Savoury Bread and Butter Pudding

Although not the most exciting dish you could imagine, this is very cheap and quick.

Serves 1   260–300 calories in each serving

3 slices wholewheat bread
75–100 g (3–4 oz) grated cheese
1 egg

150 ml (¼ pint) milk
½ teaspoon mustard powder
freshly ground black pepper

Set the oven to 200°C/400°F/Gas Mark 6. Cut the slices of bread in half, and sandwich them using most of the cheese. Cut the cheese sandwiches into pieces and put into a lightly-greased shallow ovenproof dish. Whisk the egg with the milk, mustard powder and some salt and pepper to taste. Pour over the cheese sandwiches, sprinkle with the rest of the cheese. Bake for 20–30 minutes, until puffed-up and golden brown. Serve at once. A tomato salad goes well with this.

Easy Cheese Pudding

This is one step up from the last recipe, in terms of expense, interest, and the time it takes to make! Halve the ingredients for one serving.

Serves 2–3   370–550 calories in each serving

3 slices wholewheat bread
100 g (4 oz) grated cheese
125 g (4 oz) mushrooms,
  washed and sliced
1 small green pepper, de-seeded
  and chopped

2 tomatoes, skinned and sliced
2 eggs
300 ml (½ pint) milk
1 teaspoon mustard powder
salt and freshly ground black
  pepper

Set the oven to 200°C/400°F/Gas Mark 6. Cut the slices of bread in half, and sandwich them using most of the cheese. Cut the cheese sandwiches into pieces and put into a lightly-greased shallow ovenproof dish. Put the mushrooms, pepper and tomatoes into the dish on top of the cheese sandwiches, dotting them around. Whisk the eggs with the milk, mustard powder and some salt and pepper to taste. Pour over the cheese sandwich pieces, sprinkle with the rest of the cheese. Bake for 45 minutes, until puffed-up and golden brown. Serve at once with a cooked vegetable such as frozen peas, or a crisp salad.

Tomato Bread Pudding

The third step upwards in terms of cheese pudding/bakes! It's not luxury food, but it's cheap, tasty and quite quick to make. For two portions, halve all the ingredients, but use 1 egg. Bake for 15–20 minutes.

Serves 4   330 calories in each serving

*1 large onion, peeled and
  chopped*
*1 green pepper, de-seeded and
  chopped*
25 g (1 oz) butter
*4 slices of wholewheat bread,
  crusts removed*
225 g (8 oz) can) tomatoes

*1 heaped tablespoon chopped
  parsley*
125 g (4 oz) grated cheese
1 egg
a few drops of tabasco sauce
*salt and freshly ground black
  pepper*

Set the oven to 190°C/375°F/Gas Mark 5. Fry the onion and pepper in the butter for 10 minutes. Meanwhile, mash the bread with the tomatoes, then add this to the onion mixture with the parsley, cheese, egg, tabasco and salt and pepper. Add a little milk or water if necessary to make a soft consistency. Spoon the mixture into a shallow greased dish and bake for 30 minutes.

TOAST BASE

Toasted Sandwiches

One of the cheapest and easiest snack meals. If you haven't got a sandwich toaster, toast two pieces of bread on one side, spread with the filling, grill until heated through, then sandwich them together. Here are some filling suggestions:

Cheese and Tomato: Thinly sliced or grated cheese and tomato

Cheese and Onion: Thinly sliced or grated cheese and a few thin slices of onion

Cheese and Pickle: Cheese, as above, mixed with some pickle or chutney

Avocado: Ripe avocado mashed and seasoned with salt and pepper

Mushroom: Chopped mushrooms, fried for a few minutes until tender. Allow 125 g (4 oz) for each sandwich

Tomato and Garlic: Allow 2 skinned and chopped tomatoes and a crushed garlic clove for each sandwich

Cheese on Toast

Serves 1   440–630 calories in each serving

1–2 slices wholewheat bread   *1–2 tablespoons milk*
75–100 g (3–4 oz) grated cheese   *freshly ground black pepper*

Prepare a hot grill. Toast the bread on one side. Blend the cheese to a paste with the milk, season with some pepper. Spread on the untoasted side of the bread and grill until puffed up and golden brown. Serve at once.

WHOLE LOAF BASE

Bread Pizza

This is a quick way of making a pizza and is surprisingly good. These quantities make enough for two hungry people or four not-so-hungry people. For one person, simply halve (or quarter!) all the ingredients.

Serves 4   about 570 calories in each serving

1 round or oval wholewheat
loaf, about 450g (1lb)
olive oil
2 large onions, peeled and sliced
2 garlic cloves, crushed
425 g (15 oz) can tomatoes,
   chopped

oregano
salt and freshly ground black
   pepper
125 g (4 oz) grated cheese
8 black olives

Set the oven to 220°C/425°F/Gas Mark 7. Cut the loaf in half horizontally, and scoop out some of the crumbs. Brush inside and outside the halved loaf with oil and place on a baking sheet. Fry the onions in a tablespoonful of oil for 10 minutes, then add the garlic and fry for a further minute or two. Remove from the heat and add the tomatoes and a little oregano, salt and pepper to taste. Spoon the tomato mixture onto the bread halves, sprinkle with grated cheese. Bake for 15 minutes. Serve with a green salad.

4 Choose Cheese

Cheese is a useful and very concentrated budget food. When I refer to cheese in a recipe, I mean an ordinary inexpensive Cheddar-type, though it can be a saving to buy a more expensive, well-flavoured variety, such as a matured farmhouse Cheddar, because you need much less, and so it goes further. Cheese is included in dishes in other sections in this book; the ones which follow are those which have cheese as their main ingredient.

Cheese dip

This is quick to make and, with some carrot and celery sticks to dip into it, makes a nourishing snack, or a light lunch or supper, perhaps following a soup such as the lettuce soup on page 22. For a packed lunch, put the dip into a small container such as an old yogurt pot. The mixture is quite rich, so a little goes a long way.

Serves 2–4   225–450 calories in each serving

40 g (1½ oz) soft butter
150 g (5 oz) cheese, grated fairly
   finely
6 tablespoons milk
1–2 drops tabasco sauce

salt and freshly ground black
   pepper
a little paprika pepper or a sprig
   of parsley to garnish, if
   available

Put the butter into a bowl and beat until creamy, then gradually beat in the grated cheese and milk, to make a thick, creamy mixture. Add the tabasco and a little seasoning. Spoon the mixture into a small dish to serve. It looks pretty with a sprinkling of mild red paprika pepper or a small sprig of parsley on top, if you have it.

Cheese Fondue

Cheese fondue is quick to make and always seems rather special and festive. It can be quite cheap (and very good) when made with Edam cheese and dry cider. You don't need lots of special equipment; an ordinary saucepan will do, though it's quite nice (but not essential) to have a table candle-burner if one is available, to keep the fondue hot while you dip in your bread. These quantities can be halved for a one-person serving.

Serves 2   410 calories in each serving, excluding bread

1 garlic clove, halved
7 tablespoons dry cider
225 g (8 oz) Edam cheese,
   grated
1 teaspoon cornflour
½ teaspoon lemon juice
grated nutmeg
salt and freshly ground black
   pepper

To serve

1 French stick, white or
   wholewheat, cut into
   bite-sized pieces and warmed
   in the oven

41

Rub the garlic around the inside of a medium-sized saucepan, then discard. Put 6 tablespoons of cider into the saucepan and bring just to the boil, then add the cheese and stir over a gentle heat until the cheese has melted. Mix the cornflour with the remaining tablespoonful of cider and add to the cheese mixture. Stir until slightly thickened. Remove from the heat and add the lemon juice. Season with salt, pepper and nutmeg. To eat, place the pan of fondue in the centre of the table, and use long forks to spear pieces of bread and dip them into the fondue.

Glamorgan Sausages

Quick to make, crisp little sausages which are good with a cooked vegetable or a salad. Halve the quantities for one person: double them for 4.

Serves 2–3   350–530 calories in each serving

100 g (4 oz) grated cheese
soft breadcrumbs made from 4–5
* slices of wholewheat bread,*
* crusts removed*
1 tablespoon finely grated onion

1 tablespoon chopped fresh
* parsley*
1 teaspoon made mustard
salt and freshly ground black
* pepper*

To coat

1 egg, beaten, or a few tablespoons of milk
dried breadcrumbs
oil for shallow frying

To make the sausages, mix all the ingredients together. If they seem very stiff, add a tablespoonful of water. The mixture should be firm enough to shape. Form the mixture into small sausages, dip them in beaten egg or milk, then into dried crumbs. Pour a little oil into a frying pan, to cover the base thinly, and heat. Put in the sausages and fry them, turning them with a palette knife so that they get crisp and browned all over. Drain on kitchen paper. Serve immediately.

Deep-Fried Camembert

This sounds extravagant and I suppose it is, a bit. But it's quick to do and makes a nice change. The crisp coating makes a delightful contrast with the hot runny cheese inside. Serve it with a fresh salad: a green one, or tomato and onion, and something sweet, like mango or apricot chutney. Halve the quantities for one person, and omit the tablespoonful of water.

Serves 2 well or 3 at a pinch   580–800 calories in each serving

1 box of Camembert: choose the type which has 6 individual triangles in it
1 egg, beaten with 1 tablespoon of water

dried crumbs or wheatgerm, for coating
oil for deep frying

Dip the pieces of Camembert into the egg, then into the crumbs or wheatgerm, to coat well. Have your deep-frying oil so that it fills not more than a third of the pan. Heat the oil to 190°/375°F, or so that a small cube of bread sizzles immediately it's thrown in and becomes golden brown in 1 minute. Put in the pieces of Camembert and fry for 4–5 minutes, until they are crisp and golden brown. Remove them with a draining spoon and put them on crumpled kitchen paper. Serve immediately.

5 Eggscellence

Eggs are one of the great convenience foods. A boiled, scrambled or poached egg, or an omelette, makes a very quick and nutritious meal. Here are variations on the egg theme, all quick and easy to make.

I suggest free-range eggs in the recipes; they do cost a little more, but it's good to feel that they were laid by happy hens and they've also been shown to contain a little more vitamin B12.

To hardboil eggs – needed for several of these recipes – put the eggs into a saucepan and cover with cold water. Bring to the boil, then let the eggs simmer gently for 10 minutes. Don't attempt to hardboil eggs in a microwave oven – they explode! Drain off the water, cover with cold water. Gently crack the shells by banging the eggs all over, then ease off the shell with your fingers and rinse the eggs under the cold tap to remove any small pieces of shell. A tip for preventing the eggs boiling out of their shells, which sometimes seems to happen however careful you are, is to put three or four used matchsticks into the water with the eggs. I don't know why this works, but it does!

Parsley Eggs

This is popular with children and is good with either mashed potatoes or crusty bread.

Serves 1   480 calories in each serving

For each person allow:
1–2 hardboiled eggs, cut into quarters

For the sauce

15 g (½ oz) butter or
    margarine
1 level tablespoon flour
150 ml (¼ pint) milk

25 g (1 oz) grated cheese
1 tablespoon chopped parsley
salt and freshly ground black
    pepper

Put the slices of hardboiled egg into a shallow ovenproof dish or into individual ones. Make the sauce: put the butter, flour and milk into a saucepan and whisk over a moderate heat until thickened; simmer over a gentle heat for 10 minutes. Remove from the heat and add the cheese, parsley and salt and pepper to taste. Pour over the eggs.

Egg Cheese Pie

This is a more substantial version of the last recipe, more trouble to make, but more of a meal. Serve with a cooked green vegetable, or grilled tomatoes, or frozen peas or beans. For two people, halve the quantities; for one, quarter them. Bake these smaller pies for about 20 minutes. If there's any over, mix it together, form into croquettes, coat with beaten egg and crumbs, and fry until crisp on both sides. Nice with a crisp lettuce salad.

Serves 4   590 calories in each serving

6 hardboiled eggs, shelled and chopped

For the sauce
50 g (2 oz) butter or margarine
2 heaped tablespoons flour
600 ml (1 pint) milk
125 g (4 oz) grated cheese

½ teaspoon ground mace,
  optional
salt and freshly ground black
  pepper

For the potato topping
2–3 large potatoes, peeled and
  cut into even-sized pieces

15 g (½ oz) butter
1–2 tablespoons milk

Set the oven to 190°/375°/Gas Mark 5. Next, start by making the potato topping. Put the potatoes into a saucepan, cover with cold water and bring to the boil. Boil until potatoes are tender – about 20 minutes, then drain. Dry the potatoes in the pan over the heat for a minute or two, then mash them with the butter and add enough milk to make a creamy consistency. Season with salt and pepper.

While the potatoes are cooking, make a cheese sauce. Put the butter, flour and milk into a saucepan and whisk over a moderate heat until thickened. Remove from the heat and add the cheese and salt and pepper to taste. Add the hardboiled eggs. Pour the mixture into a shallow ovenproof dish and spoon the mashed potato evenly on top. Mark the top with a fork. Bake in the oven for 30 minutes, until browned on top.

Piperade

This French version of scrambled eggs with vegetables makes a delicious and economical supper dish in the late summer when tomatoes and peppers are cheap. It's an excellent dish for one: just halve the ingredients.

Serves 2   420 calories in each serving

1 large onion, peeled and
  chopped
25 g (1 oz) butter
1 large green pepper, de-seeded
  and chopped
450 g (1 lb) tomatoes, skinned
  and chopped

1–2 cloves of garlic, crushed
4 eggs, beaten
salt and freshly ground black
  pepper

To serve
Crusty rolls or fingers of hot wholewheat toast

Fry the onion in the butter for 10 minutes, until it is soft but not browned, then add the green pepper, tomatoes and garlic and cook gently, without a lid on the pan, for a further 15–20 minutes, until the vegetables are soft but not mushy. Then pour in the beaten eggs and stir gently until the eggs begin to set. Then remove from the heat (the eggs will continue to cook in the heat of the vegetables), stir in some salt and pepper to taste and serve with the hot rolls or toast.

Spanish Omelette

These quantities can be halved for one person.

Serves 2   430 calories in each serving

2 tablespoons olive oil
1 onion, peeled and chopped
1 carrot, peeled and coarsely
  grated
1 small green pepper, de-seeded
  and chopped

225 g (8 oz) courgettes, diced
1–2 garlic cloves, crushed
4 eggs, beaten
salt and freshly ground black
  pepper

Heat the oil in a large frying pan and fry the onion, carrot and pepper, uncovered, for 5 minutes, then add the courgettes and cook for a further 5 minutes. Heat the grill. Add the garlic, beaten eggs and some seasoning to the vegetables and stir gently until the omelette begins to set. When the omelette is set underneath, place it under the grill to set the top, but don't let it get too hard. Cut in two and serve at once.

Baked Eggs

Very easy and a delicious cheap supper dish, baked eggs can be varied according to what ingredients you have available.

For each baked egg allow a little butter, a little cooked mushroom, onion, pepper or other vegetable, a spoonful of milk or cream and a little grated cheese.

Serves 1   about 300 calories in each serving

Set the oven to 190°C/375°F/Gas Mark 5. Put the cooked vegetables into little greased ovenproof dishes or ramekins and stand these in a baking tin containing hot water. Break a free-range egg into each dish, spoon over the milk or cream, season with salt and pepper and sprinkle with grated cheese. Bake for 15–20 minutes, until the eggs are set. Serve immediately with hot wholewheat toast.

VARIATION

For baked eggs in tomatoes, put all the ingredients into a large 'beefsteak' tomato which has had the inside scooped out and sprinkled with salt and pepper. Bake as described, until the egg is set and the tomato lightly cooked.

Stuffed Eggs

This is a way of making hardboiled eggs more interesting, and is a useful economical starter, light lunch or children's tea. The flavour can be varied by adding other ingredients such as a little curry powder or some chopped spring onion. Halve the ingredients if you're making it for one person.

Serves 4 as a starter, 2 as a light meal
230–460 calories in each serving

4 hardboiled eggs
1–2 tablespoons mayonnaise or
  natural yogurt
50 g (2 oz) finely-grated cheese
1–2 drops tabasco sauce
  (optional)

salt and freshly ground black
  pepper
a few lettuce leaves to serve
a little paprika pepper to
  garnish, if available

Cut the eggs in half and scoop the yolks into a bowl. Mash the egg yolks then add the mayonnaise or yogurt and cheese and mix until smooth. Add the tabasco, if you're using this, and season with salt and pepper. Spoon the mixture back into the egg whites and place on a base of lettuce. Sprinkle the yolks with a little paprika.

Egg Cutlets

For one person, simply halve the ingredients.

Serves 2   450 calories in each serving

2 eggs, beaten
6 heaped tablespoons soft
  wholewheat breadcrumbs
1 small onion, peeled and finely
  chopped
2 hardboiled eggs, chopped

4 tablespoons chopped fresh
  parsley
salt and freshly ground black
  pepper
oil for shallow frying

Add the breadcrumbs, onion, eggs and parsley to the beaten egg and season to taste. Pour enough oil into a frying pan to cover the base thinly and heat. Form the parsley mixture into burgers and fry in the oil for about 3 minutes on both sides, until crisp. Drain on kitchen paper. Serve with a salad.

Cheese Soufflé

Very easy to make, in spite of its reputation! Just make sure everyone is ready to eat it as soon as it comes out of the oven. Serve with a crisp green salad or plainly cooked vegetable. These quantities can be halved to make a soufflé for two people, and the soufflé will take about 30 minutes to cook. To make a one-person soufflé, see below.

Serves 4   300 calories in each serving

25 g (1 oz) butter	*125 g (4 oz) grated cheese*
1 heaped tablespoon flour	*4 eggs, separated*
150 ml (¼ pint) milk	*salt and freshly grated black*
½ teaspoon mustard powder	*pepper*

Set oven to 180°C/350°F/Gas Mark 4. Melt the butter in a medium-sized saucepan and stir in the flour. Mix for a moment or two, then add the milk and stir over the heat until thickened. Remove from the heat and beat in the mustard powder and cheese. Leave to cool slightly, until you can put your hand against the pan, then beat in the egg yolks and some seasoning. Whisk the whites until stiff but not so stiff that you could almost slice them with a knife. Stir a couple of tablespoons of egg white into the cheese mixture to lighten it. Using a metal spoon, fold the rest of the egg whites in. Turn the mixture into a greased soufflé dish (a 1 litre (1¾ pint) one is perfect, but any medium-sized ovenproof dish will do) and level the top. Bake for 40–45 minutes, until the soufflé is puffed-up and doesn't wobble when you shake it slightly. Serve immediately.

Individual Cheese Soufflés

These are made from the same mixture, baked in four small ovenproof dishes or ramekins for 15–20 minutes.

Cheese Soufflé for one

Follow the method above, using 15 g (½ oz) butter 1½ teaspoons of flour, 4 tablespoons of milk, a pinch of mustard, 25 g (1 oz) of grated cheese, 1 egg and salt and pepper to taste. Bake for 15 minutes. This is particularly good baked inside a large tomato (see below).

Soufflé Tomatoes

For an impressive and delicious dish, slice the tops off four large 'beefsteak' tomatoes, scoop out the pulp (you won't need it for this recipe), sprinkle the insides with salt and leave upside down to drain while you make the soufflé mixture. Then place the tomatoes in a shallow ovenproof dish, fill the cavities with cheese soufflé mixture, replace the tops as 'lids' and bake for 15–20 minutes, until the inside has puffed up and the tomatoes have cooked. Serve at once. These are particularly good served on a base of cooked spinach.

6 Better Batter

Batter, quickly made from store-cupboard ingredients, is a useful stand-by in the thrifty cook's repertoire, and found in various forms in many of the cuisines of the world. Yorkshire pudding has long been used to eke out the expensive Sunday joint – and is nourishing enough to stand on its own, with vegetables, roast potatoes and tasty gravy – and pancakes too, make a nourishing meal, either with sweet or savoury trimmings.

Old-wives tales have it that batter has to stand for an hour or so before you use it – ignore them! It's just as good when cooked straight away.

Savoury Brazil Nut Fritters

Easy to make, cheap, savoury and delicious, these puffed-up fritters are delicious with gravy and cooked vegetables, or with a sauce made by stirring some chopped chives, onion or lightly-fried sliced button mushrooms into some soured cream or plain yogurt. They're also good with chutney. For two people, use a whole egg and about 4 tablespoons of milk; halve all the other ingredients. For one person, make a two-person quantity, and freeze or keep half.

Serves 4   400 calories in each serving

4 rounded tablespoons
   self-raising wholewheat flour
1 egg
150 ml (5 fl oz) milk
100 g (4 oz) brazil nuts, roughly
   chopped
1 small onion, peeled and finely
   chopped

1 garlic clove, crushed
½ teaspoon mixed herbs
2 tablespoons chopped fresh
   parsley (if available)
salt and freshly ground black
   pepper
oil for shallow frying

Put the flour into a bowl and add the egg and milk. Beat well to make a smooth batter, then add the nuts, onion, garlic, mixed herbs, parsley if you've got it, and seasoning to taste. Pour enough oil into a frying pan to cover the base very thinly, and put over a moderate heat. When it's really hot, drop tablespoons of the batter into the frying pan, leaving a little room for them to spread. When the underside is lightly browned, and bubbles are rising to the surface of the top, flip the fritters over with a palette knife and cook the other side. Drain on kitchen paper. Serve as soon as all the fritters are done.

Mushroom Toad in the Hole

This is delicious made with field mushrooms, should you be able to lay your hands on some. Otherwise choose the largest and most open mushrooms you can find. Use a baking tin to cook this in (rather than a casserole dish) because it conducts the heat better and makes the batter puffy and crisp. For two people, halve all the ingredients and bake for 25–30 minutes; for one person, use 1 egg, 4 tablespoons of milk and a quarter of all the other ingredients. Bake for 15–20 minutes.

Serves 4   310 calories in each serving

225 g (8 oz) open mushrooms
  or field mushrooms
4 tablespoons oil
4 rounded tablespoons plain
  85% wholewheat flour

½ teaspoon salt
2 eggs
300 ml (½ pint) milk

Set the oven to 220°C/425°F/Gas Mark 7. Wash the mushrooms and peel off the skins if you're using field ones. Cut into even-sized pieces. Heat 2 tablespoons of the oil in a saucepan and fry the mushrooms for 2–3 minutes on each side. Drain. Put the flour and salt into a large bowl, make a well in the middle and break in the eggs. Add half the milk and mix well, gradually mixing in all the flour and adding the rest of the milk. Put the remaining 2 tablespoons of oil into a baking tin and heat in the oven until smoking hot, then pour in the batter and pop the mushrooms in on top. Bake for 35 minutes, until puffed up and golden brown. A tasty gravy, mashed potatoes and a cooked vegetable such as cabbage or carrots go well with this. I also think it's nice with a crisp green salad.

Savoury Olive Mushroom Cake

This recipe was given to me by a French friend. If, like me, you like olives, you'll love it! A half quantity of this also works well, baked for about 30 minutes, for two people, as does a quarter quantity, baked in a small dish or tin for 15–20 minutes, for one person. If you haven't any left-over white wine, water will do, but the wine gives a subtle, fruity flavour.

Serves 4   590 calories in each serving

250 g (10 oz) (10 heaped
*   tablespoons) self-raising 85%*
*   wholewheat flour*
pinch of salt
4 eggs

150 ml (5 fl oz) white wine
4 tablespoons olive oil
225 g (8 oz) stoned green olives
175 g (6 oz) sliced mushrooms
175 g (6 oz) grated cheese

Set the oven to 250°C/500°F/Gas Mark 9. Grease a cake or bread tin. Put the flour and salt into a bowl and add the eggs, wine and oil. Mix until smooth, then add the olives, mushrooms and grated cheese. Spoon the mixture into the prepared tin. Bake for 10 minutes, then turn down the oven setting to 190°C/375°F/Gas Mark 5 and bake for a further 40–50 minutes.

Pancakes

Pancakes are easy and fun to make and can be served simply with sugar and lemon, or with some grated cheese, soured cream or cheese sauce. Or they can be rolled round all kinds of different fillings – left-over vegetables are great for this – and served as they are, or with some cheese sauce or grated cheese on top and browned in the oven or under the grill. For a special cheap but tasty meal, they can be stacked up flat on top of each other, with filling in between, covered with cheese sauce, and cut into wedges, like a cake.

Basic Pancakes

These quantities can easily be halved to make the right amount for one or two people.

Makes about 1 dozen   80 calories in each pancake

4 rounded tablespoons plain 85% or 100% wholewheat flour
½ teaspoon salt
2 eggs

150 ml (5 fl oz) milk
150 ml (5 fl oz) water
2 tablespoons melted butter
extra butter for frying

Put the flour and salt into a bowl, mix in the eggs, then gradually add the milk, water and butter to make a smooth, fairly thin batter. Heat 7 g (¼ oz) of butter in a small frying pan; when it sizzles, pour off the excess, so that the frying pan is just glistening. Keep the frying pan over a high heat, give the pancake batter a quick stir, then put two tablespoonfuls into the frying pan and tip it to make the batter run all over the bottom. Cook the pancake for about 30 seconds, until the top is set and the underneath is tinged with golden brown. Remove the pancake with a palette knife and put it onto a plate. Make about a dozen more pancakes in the same way, piling them up on top of each other on the plate.

SWEET IDEAS

Sugar and Lemon: Sprinkle pancakes with sugar and serve with lemon slices.

Honey or Golden Syrup: Pour the warmed honey or golden syrup over the pancakes and serve with lemon slices.

Jam and Yogurt or Cream: Spread the pancakes with warmed jam and serve with natural yogurt or fresh or soured cream.

Orange Butter Cream: Beat together equal quantities of soft butter and soft brown sugar, flavour with grated orange rind.

Chocolate Pancakes: Replace a tablespoonful of the flour in the batter with a tablespoonful of cocoa. Serve with whipped cream and a sprinkling of sugar.

Fruity Filling: Spread the pancakes with stewed apples, rhubarb or other fruit (see pages 177–78), sprinkle with sugar, and serve with yogurt or cream if you like.

SAVOURY SUGGESTIONS

The pancakes can be filled and served as they are, or they can be filled, packed side by side into a shallow ovenproof dish, covered with a well-flavoured cheese or tomato sauce, a little cream or a layer of grated cheese, and baked in a moderate oven (190°C/375°F/Gas Mark 5) for 45 minutes for a four-person quantity, 30 minutes for a two-person bake, and 15–20 minutes for one. Serve with a simple cooked vegetable to contrast with the filling and mashed potatoes as well for a filling meal.

These quantities are enough to fill pancakes for four people but the quantities can easily be halved or quartered.

Spinach: This makes a very good filling for pancakes. Wash 900 g/2 lb fresh spinach. Remove and chop the stalks unless they're very tender, roughly chop the leaves. Heat 6 cm (¼ inch) of water in a large saucepan and put in the stalks. Boil for 4–5 minutes, until the stalks are nearly tender, then drain off the water and put the leaves in on top. Cook for a further 5–8 minutes, until the leaves are tender. It helps to push down and 'chop' the spinach using the end of a fish slice. Drain well. Add a knob of butter and salt, pepper and grated nutmeg to taste. Spinach pancakes are good served with cheese sauce.

Cabbage Special: Fry a chopped onion in 25 g (1 oz) butter for 10 minutes, then add 450 g (1 lb) shredded cabbage, a crushed garlic clove, 2 skinned and chopped tomatoes (canned are fine) and some salt and pepper. Cook gently, stirring often, until the cabbage is tender – about 10 minutes. Flavour with a little grated nutmeg or some caraway seeds. Stuff the pancakes and serve as they are, or covered with cheese sauce or a little soured cream.

Carrot and Ginger: Mix 450 g (1 lb) cooked, diced carrot with 1 onion which has been chopped and fried for 10 minutes in 25 g (1 oz) butter with a walnut-sized knob of fresh ginger, grated. Season with salt and pepper. Other root vegetables such as swede and parsnip can also be used, perhaps replacing some of the carrot.

Red Kidney Bean and Tomato: Fry a chopped onion in 25 g (1 oz) butter for 10 minutes, then add the drained contents of a 425 g (15 oz) can of red kidney beans, or 125 g (4 oz) dried red kidney beans, soaked, cooked and drained, (see page 141) a 425 g (15 oz) can of tomatoes, a crushed garlic clove and some salt and pepper. Cook until heated through. Again, these stuffed pancakes are good covered with cheese sauce or some soured cream.

Courgette or Marrow and Cheese: Fry a chopped onion in 25 g (1 oz) butter for 10 minutes, then add 750 g (1½ lb) diced courgette or marrow and cook gently for about 10 minutes, until tender. Stir in 125 g (4 oz) grated cheese. Pancakes filled with this are nice just as they are, or covered with a tomato sauce.

Mushroom: Fry a chopped onion in 25 g (1 oz) butter for 10 minutes, then add 450 g (1 lb) washed and chopped mushrooms and fry for a further 3–4 minutes to cook the mushrooms. Then add 2 skinned and chopped tomatoes and stir over a gentle heat until the tomato has warmed through. Season with salt, pepper and nutmeg. Pancakes filled with this can be sprinkled with grated cheese and browned in the oven or under the grill, or served as they are.

Ratatouille: This makes an excellent filling for pancakes when the ingredients are in season and you can make it cheaply. Follow the recipe on page 88–9. Cover filled pancakes with grated cheese, soured cream or cheese sauce.

Sweetcorn: Cook 450 g (1 lb) fresh or frozen sweetcorn kernels in a little boiling water, drain and add 150 ml (5 fl oz) soured cream or a little cheese sauce, to bind, and salt and pepper to taste. Top with a little grated cheese.

Tomato and Onion: Fry a large chopped onion in 25 g (1 oz) butter for 10 minutes, then add 450 g (1 lb) skinned and chopped tomatoes and stir over the heat until the tomatoes have heated through. Season with salt and pepper. 1–2 tablespoons of chopped basil are nice added to this when available. Top these pancakes with a little grated cheese, soured cream or a cheese or mushroom sauce.

Potato and Pea: Mix 450 g (1 lb) diced boiled potatoes and 100 g (4 oz) peas (left-overs are ideal) with a chopped and fried onion. A tablespoonful of grated fresh ginger or some chopped parsley are good in this and soured cream or grated cheese makes a nice topping.

7 Fasta Pasta

The all-time favourite 'fast food', as long as it isn't overcooked, pasta is good almost any way. A big bowlful of pasta served with just butter, salt and freshly ground black pepper, and a sprinkling of Parmesan if the budget allows, makes a comforting meal when you're very hard up, and it's nourishing, filling and high in fibre. It's interesting to try the different shapes, and sometimes to mix green and white pastas, perhaps intensifying the colour contrast by stirring in some chopped fresh dark green herbs, too. And left-over pasta can be made into a good salad.

If you like sauce with your pasta, it's a good idea to make up a double batch of a favourite, such as the fresh tomato, or the lentil and herb, and store half of it in the fridge or freezer for another day.

How To Cook Pasta Perfectly

The first essential is to use your largest saucepan, because pasta needs to be able to move around in the water so that it doesn't stick together and come out in a solid mass. Fill the pan two thirds full with water, add a couple of teaspoons of salt, and bring to the boil. When the water reaches a rolling boil, throw in your pasta, or, if it's spaghetti, hold it in your hand like a bunch of flowers, stand the base of the 'stems' in the water, and gently push them down into the water as they soften, until it's all in. Then give the pasta a quick stir, and let it boil away, without a lid, until it's done. This will take anything from about 7 minutes to 15, depending on the size of the pieces. The packet will give a guide, but fish a piece of pasta out with a perforated spoon and bite it just before the time is up, to see how it's doing. It should be tender but nowhere near soggy. As soon as it reaches this stage, drain it. The easiest way to do this is to use a metal colander, stand it squarely in the sink and pour all the pasta and water into it. Give the colander a good shake, to dislodge all the water, then pop the pasta back into the saucepan and add a knob of butter and some salt and freshly ground black pepper. Serve at once, before it has a chance to cool down, as it is, or with any other trimmings you may have.

If you're serving pasta as a main meal, without much else, two hungry people will probably happily get through 350 g (12 oz); otherwise, allow 175–250 g (6–8 oz) for two.

SIMPLE ADDITIONS FOR PASTA

You can turn hot cooked pasta into a feast very simply by adding other ingredients:

Pasta with Fresh Herbs

Just add a tablespoonful or so of chopped fresh herbs to the buttery cooked pasta. Tarragon and basil are delicious.

Creamy Pasta

A luxury one for special occasions, stir a little double cream into the hot cooked pasta, allowing a couple of tablespoons per person. (This isn't nearly as wicked, fatty or extravagant as it sounds when you consider how much cheese people often put over their pasta – quite virtuous, in comparison, in fact!).

Cheesy Pasta

Sprinkle the pasta with a little dry grated cheese. Cheddar which has been left uncovered in the fridge or cupboard to dry out, for rock-bottom prices, Parmesan if you can afford it. Parmesan is nicest if you can buy a small piece and keep it in the fridge to grate as you need it. Grate it on the fine side of the grater; it's very hard, and is expensive, but a little goes a long way.

Pasta with Avocado

A small ripe avocado, peeled and chopped, and added to the hot cooked pasta after draining, will heat through a little in the heat of the pasta and the buttery flavour and texture goes well with pasta.

Pasta with Nuts

A few chopped, very fresh, walnuts go beautifully with hot cooked pasta. They're nicest if you buy them in the shell and crack a few while the pasta cooks. Chop them roughly and add to the drained and buttered pasta. A little cream mixed in as well makes this really special.

Pasta with Beans and Black Olives

While the pasta is cooking, heat through a can of cannellini beans in another saucepan. Drain both the beans and the pasta and mix together with a little crushed garlic, a tablespoonful or so of olive oil and a few whole black olives. If you want to be even more elaborate, you can add a skinned and chopped tomato and some chopped parsley.

Pasta with Chick Peas

An old Italian favourite, this is just hot drained chick peas, canned or home-cooked, added to hot cooked pasta, with some olive oil to make the whole lot glossy, and plenty of crushed garlic.

Pasta with Croutons

While the pasta is cooking, cut a slice of wholewheat bread for each person, cut off the crusts, and cut the bread into 6 mm (¼ inch) squares. Heat a little olive oil in a frying pan, and fry the bread croutons until crisp and golden brown all over. Drain on kitchen paper. Add the croutons to each bowl of hot pasta.

Pasta with Onions

Start this when you put the water for the pasta on to boil, to give the onions time to cook until they're really soft and slightly caramelized. Allow ½–1 large onion for each person, peeled and sliced. Heat a knob of butter in a saucepan or frying pan and put in the onion. Fry for 10 minutes, then add a sprinkling of salt, pepper and sugar, and continue to fry for a further 5–10 minutes, until the onion is golden brown but not burnt. Stir the hot, cooked onion into the cooked and drained pasta.

PASTA WITH SAUCES

One step up from just adding tasty ingredients to the cooked pasta, is to make a sauce to pour on top of it. This needn't be a complicated affair; the tomato sauce, the tomato and mushroom sauce and the creamy mushroom sauce can all be made while the pasta cooks.

Fresh Tomato Sauce

Allow about a tablespoonful of finely chopped onion and 2 good-sized tomatoes for each person. Skin and chop the tomatoes. Fry the onion in a knob of butter in a medium-sized pan for 5 minutes, then put in the tomato and a crushed garlic clove, and fry gently for a further 5 minutes or so, until both the tomato and the onion are tender. Season with salt and pepper. Serve this as it is, poured over the hot cooked pasta, or liquidize first. If you're making this for a family, and want to make it more cheaply, you can use a 425 g (15 oz) can of tomatoes; they don't taste so fresh, but are fine, if well-flavoured with the onion and garlic.

Fresh Tomato and Mushroom Sauce

Make in the same way as the above, adding 25–50 g (1–2 oz) of washed and finely chopped button mushrooms with the tomatoes.

Mushroom Sauce

Allow 125 g (4 oz) mushrooms for each person. Wash and chop the mushrooms, then fry them lightly in a little butter for 4–5 minutes, until tender. Add 2 tablespoons of soured cream or plain yogurt, or double cream, and some salt, pepper, crushed garlic and freshly grated nutmeg if you have it.

Nutty Sauce

You need a liquidizer, food processor or some patience with a pestle and mortar for this one. For two servings, crush 1 garlic clove, then add 50 g (2 oz) walnuts (or pine kernels, if you're feeling extravagant), a pinch of dried thyme, a pinch each of salt, pepper and sugar. When it's all fairly smooth and thick, gradually mix in 2–3 tablespoons milk or cream. Add this to the hot cooked pasta and mix with a fork so that the sauce coats all the pasta, then serve.

Tagliatelle Verde with Lentil Sauce

This sauce takes a bit longer to make than the sauces above, but is cheap, tasty and turns cooked spaghetti into a very filling, welcoming meal. For one or two people, halve the ingredients, using a 225 g (8 oz) can of tomatoes. For one, it's probably best to make a half quantity and freeze what you don't need, or keep it in the fridge for a day or two for another meal.

Serves 4   470–570 calories in each serving, excluding cheese

225–350 g (8–12 oz) tagliatelle
15 g (½ oz) butter

For the sauce:

*1 large onion, peeled and
    chopped*
2 tablespoons oil
2 garlic cloves, crushed
½ teaspoon cinnamon

*225 g (8 oz) split red lentils,
    washed*
400 g (14 oz) can tomatoes
400 ml (¾ pint) water
*salt and freshly ground black
    pepper*

To serve:

grated cheese

Start making the sauce. Fry the onion in the oil for 10 minutes, then add the garlic, cinnamon, lentils, tomatoes and water and bring up to the boil. Let the mixture simmer gently for about 20 minutes, until the lentils are tender; taste and season with salt and pepper. While the lentil sauce is cooking, cook the tagliatelle as described above. Put the cooked tagliatelle in a large warmed serving dish and pour the sauce into the centre. Offer grated cheese separately.

Pasta with Green Lentils and Tomatoes

Halve these quantities for one person.

Serves 3   470–600 calories in each serving

225–350 g (8–12 oz) spaghetti
15g (½ oz) butter

For the sauce:

125 g (4 oz) green lentils
water
15 g (½ oz) butter
1 large onion, peeled and
* chopped*
1 garlic clove, crushed
1 teaspoon dried basil, or 1
* tablespoon chopped fresh*
* basil*

225 g (8 oz) tomatoes, skinned
* and chopped, or a 225 g (8*
* oz) can*
salt and freshly ground black
* pepper*

To serve:

grated cheese

First make the sauce. Put the lentils into a large saucepan with the water and boil gently until tender, about 45 minutes. Drain. Meanwhile melt the butter in a large saucepan and fry the onion until tender. Add the garlic, basil if you're using dried, tomatoes and drained lentils. Season with salt and pepper. While the lentil sauce is cooking, cook the spaghetti as described above. Reheat the sauce, adding the basil if you're using fresh. Put the cooked spaghetti in a large warmed serving dish and pour the sauce into the centre. Offer grated cheese separately.

PASTA BAKES

In these, cooked pasta is combined with other ingredients, then baked before serving. A crunchy green salad goes well with them, or a quickly-cooked vegetable such as broccoli or frozen peas.

Macaroni Cheese

An always-popular old favourite, with a tangy sauce. These quantities will halve satisfactorily to make enough for two; for one person, use 50 g (2 oz) macaroni, 15 g (½ oz) butter, 2 rounded teaspoons of flour, 200 ml (7 fl oz) milk, ½ teaspoonful of mustard and 40 g (1½ oz) grated cheese.

Serves 4   510–780 calories in each serving

225 g (8 oz) macaroni
50 g (2 oz) butter
2 rounded tablespoons flour
800 ml (1½ pints) milk
2 teaspoons made mustard

175 g (6 oz) grated cheese
salt and freshly ground black
*   pepper*
6 heaped tablespoons
*   wholewheat breadcrumbs*

Fill a large saucepan three quarters full of water, add a teaspoonful of salt and bring to the boil. Then add the macaroni and cook for 8–10 minutes, without a lid on the pan, until the macaroni is just tender. Drain macaroni into a colander. While the macaroni is cooking, make the sauce. Melt the butter in a saucepan then add the flour; stir for a moment or two over the heat, then stir in the milk, a quarter at a time, stirring well and allowing the sauce to thicken between each lot of milk. Leave the sauce to simmer gently over the heat for 5 minutes, then remove from the heat and add the mustard, two thirds of the grated cheese and salt and pepper to taste. Heat the grill, or turn the oven to 200°C/400°F/Gas Mark 6. Add the macaroni to the sauce and stir well, then spoon the mixture into a large shallow ovenproof dish. Sprinkle the crumbs and the remaining cheese over the top. Grill for 5–10 minutes, or heat through in the oven for about 20 minutes, until the top is golden brown and crisp and the inside bubbling. Serve with a crisp salad.

Macaroni Bake

Another variation on the theme, this is tasty, can be prepared in advance for baking later, and also freezes well. Some cooked frozen peas or a crisp green salad go well with it. For two servings, halve all the ingredients but use a whole egg. Make this quantity for one, and freeze what you don't need, or keep the remainder in the fridge for another day, perhaps as a stuffing for a green pepper – prepared as described on page 102, stuffed, then baked for about 15 minutes.

Serves 4   320 calories in each serving

125 g (4 oz) macaroni
2 onions, peeled and chopped
1 tablespoon oil
125 g (4 oz) mushrooms,
  washed and chopped
225 g (8 oz) tomatoes, skinned
  and chopped

1 egg, beaten
125 g (4 oz) grated cheese
salt and freshly ground black
  pepper
a few wholewheat breadcrumbs
  for topping

Fill a large saucepan two thirds full of water, add a teaspoonful of salt and bring to the boil. Then put in the macaroni, stir, and let it simmer, without a lid on the pan, for about 10 minutes, until a piece feels just tender when you bite it. Drain immediately. The easiest way to do this is to pour it into a metal colander. Set the oven to 190°C/375°F/Gas Mark 5. While the macaroni is cooking, fry the onions in the oil for 7 minutes, then add the mushrooms and tomatoes and cook for a further 3 minutes. Beat in the egg and stir over the heat for a moment or two longer until the egg begins to set. Remove from the heat and add the macaroni, cheese and some salt and pepper to taste. Spoon the mixture into a shallow ovenproof dish, sprinkle crumbs over the top and bake for 25–30 minutes, until the top is crisp and golden brown.

Pasta with Leeks and Cheese

An easy pasta dish which can be made in a quarter or half portion for one or two people.

Serves 4   450 calories in each serving

225 g (8 oz) wholewheat pasta rings
4 leeks, trimmed, washed and cut into 1 cm (½ inch) pieces

175 g (6 oz) grated cheese
Salt and freshly ground black pepper

Fill a large saucepan two thirds full of water, add a teaspoonful of salt and bring to the boil. Then put in the pasta rings, stir, and let them simmer, without a lid on the pan, for about 10 minutes, until a piece of pasta feels just tender when you bite it. Drain immediately. While the pasta is cooking, prepare the leeks. To do this, put 1 cm (½ inch) of water into a saucepan and when it boils, put in the leeks. Boil for 4–5 minutes, until just tender, then drain well. Prepare a hot grill. Grease the grill pan or a shallow dish which will fit under the grill. Put the pasta into this in an even layer, then put the leeks in on top. Season with some pepper. Sprinkle the cheese over the top and grill until the cheese has melted and is golden brown. Serve immediately. A tomato salad goes well with this.

Pasta, Tomatoes, Onions and Cheese

For two servings, halve all the quantities, using a 225 g (8 oz) can of tomatoes; for one person, use a quarter of the quantities and half a 225 g (8 oz) can of tomatoes.

Serves 4   430 calories in each serving

225 g (8 oz) macaroni or
   wholewheat pasta rings
2 large onions, peeled and sliced
2 tablespoons oil
425 g (15 oz) can tomatoes

salt and freshly ground black
   pepper
125 g (4 oz) grated cheese

Fill a large saucepan two thirds full of water, add a teaspoonful of salt and bring to the boil. Then put in the pasta rings, stir, and let them simmer, without a lid on the pan, for about 10 minutes, until a piece of pasta feels just tender when you bite it. Drain immediately. While the pasta is cooking, prepare the tomato mixture. Fry the onions in the oil in a large saucepan for 10 minutes, until tender, then add the tomatoes, mashing them a bit to break them up. Season with salt and pepper. Prepare a hot grill. Grease the grill pan or a shallow dish which will fit under the grill. Put the pasta into this in an even layer, then pour the tomato mixture on top and sprinkle with the cheese. A few black olives tucked in amongst the pasta are nice, if you have them. Put under the grill until the cheese has melted and is golden brown. Serve immediately. A crisp green salad goes well with this.

PASTA SALADS

These are a good way of using up some left-over cooked pasta, but they're also worth making specially, because they make a pleasant, filling meal. Just add some vinaigrette, cream, plain yogurt or mayonnaise to the cooked pasta, then put in some colourful and varied ingredients to make the salad tasty and interesting. Here are some pleasant mixtures:

Macaroni and Tomato Salad

This is cooked macaroni, black olives, finely chopped onion and chopped skinned tomatoes, dressed with some vinaigrette.

Pasta Shells with Carrot and Raisins

Cooked, well-drained pasta shells, mixed with coarsely grated carrots and some raisins, with mayonnaise, yogurt or soured cream to bind. Some cooked sweetcorn kernels are good in this, too, either instead of, or as well as, the raisins.

Two-Colour Pasta and Herb Salad

Cook equal quantities of green and white pasta twists, drain well. Dress with vinaigrette and add plenty of fresh chopped herbs.

Nutty Pasta Salad

Dress the hot pasta with the nutty mixture on page 65; cool. This makes a delicious salad and is particularly good made with green and white pasta twists.

8 Speedy Spuds

Potatoes are one of the cornerstones of cheap and easy cookery. They're economical to buy, quick to prepare and packed with nutrients. And if you add just small quantities of more concentrated foods such as milk, cheese or nuts, they make nourishing main courses which are popular with most people.

BAKED POTATO BASE

For baked potatoes, simply scrub one or two large potatoes per person, prick and bake at 230°C/450°F/Gas Mark 8 for 1–1½ hours, until the potatoes feel soft when squeezed and the skins are crisp. Then split open and serve with butter and grated cheese, or some cottage cheese or soured cream or plain yogurt, or with one of the following toppings:

Toppings for Baked Potatoes

Mushroom and Soured Cream

Enough for 4 potatoes   350 calories in each serving

15 g (½ oz) butter
125 g (4 oz) button mushrooms,
   washed and sliced

150 ml (6 fl oz) carton soured
   cream

First prepare the sauce. Fry the mushrooms in the butter for 2–3 minutes, until just softened, then stir in the soured cream and salt and pepper to taste. Heat gently – don't boil – serve poured over the split potato halves.

Creamy Sweetcorn

Enough for 4 potatoes   320 calories in each serving

100 g (4 oz) frozen sweetcorn
   kernels
4 tablespoons cream

salt and freshly ground black
   pepper

Put the sweetcorn into a saucepan with the cream, mashing the sweetcorn slightly. Stir over the heat until the sweetcorn is hot. Pour over the split potato halves. Season to taste.

Chilli-Tomato-Cheese

*Enough for 4 potatoes   470 calories in each serving, including a
300g (10 oz) potato*

15 g (½ oz) butter
*1 small onion, peeled and
  chopped*
225 g (8 oz) can tomatoes

½ teaspoon chilli powder
125 g (4 oz) grated cheese

Melt the butter in a medium-sized saucepan and fry the onion in the
butter for 10 minutes, until soft but not browned. Then add the
tomatoes, mashing them a bit as you put them in, and the chilli
powder and grated cheese. Stir gently over the heat until the cheese
has melted and the mixture is hot. Pour over the split potato halves.

Stuffed Jacket Potatoes

Serve these with some salad, such as one of the cabbage salads or
the crunchy carrot salad.

Serves 1   420–540 calories in each serving

1 or 2 large potatoes per person
25–50 g (1–2oz) cheese
*a little butter and milk per
  person*

seasoning to taste

Scrub and prick the potatoes, then bake them at 230°F/450°F/Gas
Mark 8 for 1–1½ hours until the skins are crisp and the potatoes
feel tender inside when squeezed. Halve the potatoes and scoop out
the insides. Place the skins on a baking tray. Mash the scooped-out
potato with a little butter and milk, half the grated cheese and some
salt and pepper. Pile the mixture back into the skins, sprinkle with
the remaining grated cheese and put the potatoes back into the oven
for about 20 minutes, until golden brown and crisp.

RAW POTATO BASE

These dishes start with raw peeled potatoes which are then grated
and fried as quick potato pancakes or pizza base; or they are sliced
and fried with other tasty ingredients, until tender, or sliced and
layered in a shallow casserole with cheese and onion and baked.

Potato and Onion Fry

Very simple, cheap and filling.

Serves 2 as a main meal   340 calories in each serving

1 onion, peeled and sliced
2 tablespoons oil
2 large potatoes, peeled and cut
    into even-sized pieces

salt and freshly ground black
    pepper

Fry the onion in a large saucepan in the oil for 5 minutes, then add
the potatoes, sprinkle with a little salt, stir and cook over a very
gentle heat for 15–20 minutes, until the potatoes are tender and
lightly-browned, stirring quite often to prevent sticking. Serve at
once.

Potatoes with Peppers, Onions and Tomatoes

This is really a more elaborate version of the above recipe, with
tomatoes, garlic and green pepper added to give extra flavour and
interest. It's delicious served with a spoonful of soured cream or
plain yogurt. Halve these quantities for one serving, using a 225 g
(8 oz) can of tomatoes.

Serves 2–3 as a main meal   320–480 calories in each serving

1 onion, peeled and sliced
1 green pepper, de-seeded and
   sliced
2 tablespoons oil
2 large potatoes, peeled and cut
   into even-sized pieces

425 g (15 oz) can tomatoes
2–3 teaspoons mild paprika
   pepper
salt and freshly ground black
   pepper

Fry the onion and pepper in a large saucepan in the oil for 5 minutes, then add the tomatoes and potatoes, sprinkle with a little salt, stir, and cook over a very gentle heat for 15–20 minutes, until the potatoes are tender, stirring quite often to prevent sticking. Stir in the paprika pepper and salt and pepper to taste as necessary. Serve at once.

Potato and Cheese Layer

This is very quick and easy to make and popular with children; you need to allow time for it to cook slowly in a cool oven. It's nice with a plainly cooked green vegetable or some watercress. For one person, halve the quantities – if there's some over, it makes a good stuffing for a large tomato.

Serves 2–4 as a main course   450–690 calories in each serving

25 g (1 oz) butter
2 large potatoes, peeled and
   thinly sliced
2 medium-sized onions, peeled
   and thinly sliced

125 g (4 oz) cheese
4 tablespoons milk
salt and freshly ground black
   pepper

Set the oven to 170°C/325°F/Gas Mark 3. Grease a shallow ovenproof dish using half the butter. Put a layer of potatoes in the bottom of the dish, then a thin layer of onion slices, a little grated cheese, salt and pepper. Continue in layers like this until all the ingredients are used, ending with potato. Pour the milk over the top and dot with butter.

Bake for about 1½ hours, until the potato feels tender when pierced with a sharp knife or skewer.

VARIATION

This is good with some mushrooms added. Just wash and slice a few mushrooms – 50–100 g (2–4 oz) – and layer with the onion.

Easy Potato Pancake

Another potato dish which is popular as a children's tea. Halve the ingredients for one person.

Serves 2–4   300–590 calories in each serving

2 large potatoes, scrubbed
1 medium-sized onion, peeled
salt and freshly ground black
  pepper

2 eggs
3 tablespoons wholewheat flour
oil for shallow frying

Grate the potatoes coarsely (there's no need to peel them), then grate the onion and mix with the potatoes, together with some salt and pepper to taste, the eggs and flour, to make a batter. Heat a little oil in a frying pan and fry tablespoonfuls of the mixture until golden and crispy, turning them over so that both sides are cooked. Drain on kitchen paper and serve.

Even Easier Potato Pancake

This is one big pancake which you then cut into wedges, and serve as an accompanying dish, or with a salad for a light meal. Or you can cover the cooked pancake with sliced tomatoes and grated cheese, grill or bake until the cheese melts and browns, and serve as an unusual (and very popular) pizza.

Serves 2   430 calories in each serving

2 large potatoes, scrubbed   oil for shallow frying
salt and freshly ground black
   pepper

Grate the potatoes coarsely (there's no need to peel them), then season them with salt and pepper. Put enough oil in a frying pan to cover the base thinly, and heat. When the oil is really hot, put in all the potato and press it down to make a flat round shape. Fry until the base is crispy and golden brown, then flip the pancake over with a fish slice and fry the other side. Drain well, blot with kitchen paper. Serve at once.

Potato Pizza

Serves 2 as main meal   700 calories in each serving

2 large potatoes, scrubbed   optional garnishes
salt and freshly ground black
   pepper   A few slices of mushroom or
oil for shallow frying   green pepper, or a few black
                                         olives.
For the topping
2 large tomatoes, sliced
125 g (4 oz) grated cheese

Make the potato cake exactly as described in the previous recipe. While you're cooking the pancake, heat the grill or oven (230°C/450°F/Gas Mark 8). Put the pancake onto a heatproof plate, put the tomatoes on top in an even layer, sprinkle with grated cheese. Arrange any garnishes on top. Grill or bake for 10–15 minutes, until the cheese has melted and is golden brown. Serve at once.

Potato Hotpot

In this tasty family dish the raw potatoes are parboiled for 10 minutes before layering into the casserole. Halve the quantities for two people, using a 225 g (8 oz) can of tomatoes. For one person, it's worth making a half quantity and freezing or keeping what you don't need.

Serves 4   540 calories in each serving

*2 large potatoes, peeled and
  sliced
2 onions, peeled and sliced
425 g (15 oz) can tomatoes
300 g (½ pint) cheese sauce (see
  page 28)*

*dried basil, celery salt, freshly
  ground black pepper
3–4 tablespoons grated cheese
a little butter or margarine*

Set oven to 180°C/350°F/Gas Mark 4. Boil the potatoes for 10 minutes, then drain. Arrange layers of potato, onion, tomato and cheese sauce in a greased heatproof dish, seasoning between each layer with basil, pepper and celery salt, and finishing with a layer of potato. Sprinkle with the grated cheese, dot with butter or margarine and cook for 45 minutes. A simply cooked green vegetable goes well with this.

Speedy Cheesy Mash

Incredibly easy and cheap, this is good with some sliced tomato or watercress, or a quickly-cooked vegetable. Quarter or halve these quantities for one or two servings.

Serves 4   500 calories in each serving

*4 large potatoes, peeled and cut   100 g (4 oz) grated cheese
   into even-sized pieces   1 tomato, thinly sliced
25 g (1 oz) butter
2–3 tablespoons milk*

Put the potatoes into a saucepan, cover with cold water and bring to the boil. Boil until potatoes are tender – about 20 minutes – then drain. Dry the potatoes in the pan over the heat for a minute or two, then mash them with half the butter and add enough milk to make a creamy consistency. Stir in half the grated cheese and season with salt and pepper. Heat the grill. Spread the mixture into the grill pan, or a shallow heatproof dish which will fit under the grill. Sprinkle with the rest of the cheese, arrange the tomato slices on top and dot with the remaining butter. Grill for about 10 minutes, until golden brown on top and hot inside.

COOKED POTATO BASE

These dishes can be quickly prepared if you have some left-over boiled or mashed potatoes: you can save time by planning for them in advance and cooking extra potato for a previous meal. Quarter or halve the quantities for one or two servings.

Nutty Potato Cakes

Serves 4   800 calories in each serving

4 large potatoes, peeled and cut
  into even-sized pieces
15 g (½ oz) butter
2–3 tablespoons milk
100 g (4 oz) roughly-chopped
  nuts: any kind, roasted
  peanuts are cheapest

2 heaped tablespoons chopped
  parsley (if available)
wholewheat flour for coating
oil gor shallow frying

Put the potatoes into a saucepan, cover with cold water and bring
to the boil. Boil until potatoes are tender – about 20 minutes – then
drain. Dry the potatoes in the pan over the heat for a minute or
two, then mash them with the butter and add enough milk to make
a creamy consistency. Stir in the chopped nuts and parsley, if
available, season with salt and pepper. Form into potato cakes, coat
in wholewheat flour. Pour enough oil into a frying pan to coat the
base lightly and set over a moderate heat. When the oil is hot, put
in the potato cakes and fry until brown on one side, then turn them
over and fry the other side. Serve with a tomato, carrot or cabbage
salad, buttered spinach or grilled tomatoes and mushrooms.

Potato and Mushroom Au Gratin

Halve the ingredients to make the right amount to serve two
people; for one person, either do this, and freeze or keep half, or use
the following quantities: 1 large potato, 25 g (1 oz) butter, 50 g (2
oz) mushrooms, 2 rounded teaspoons flour and 150 ml (¼ pint)
milk.

Serves 4   540 calories in each serving

4 large potatoes, peeled and cut
   into even-sized pieces
65 g (2½ oz) butter
175 g (6 oz) mushrooms,
   washed and sliced

2 rounded tablespoons flour
575 ml (1 pint) milk
salt, pepper and ground mace

Put the potatoes into a saucepan, cover with cold water and bring
to the boil. Boil until potatoes are tender – about 20 minutes – then
drain. Meanwhile melt 50 g (2 oz) of the butter and fry the
mushrooms for 2 minutes. Then stir in the flour and milk and stir
vigorously over the heat until smooth and thickened; leave to
simmer gently for 5–10 minutes, to cook the flour. Season with salt,
pepper and a pinch or so of mace. Heat the grill. Add the potatoes
to the mushroom mixture, check seasoning. Pour the mixture into
the grill pan, or a shallow heatproof dish which will fit under the
grill. Level the top, dot with the remaining butter. Grill for about
10 minutes, until golden brown on top and hot inside. A crisp green
salad goes well with this, or some cooked peas or carrots.

Potato Salad

Serves 2 as a lunch, 4 as an accompaniment to a main dish
300–600 calories in each serving, using half yogurt and half
mayonnaise

2 large potatoes
3 heaped tablespoons real
   mayonnaise or mayonnaise
   and plain yogurt mixed
salt and freshly ground black
   pepper

a few lettuce leaves and some
   chopped spring onion to
   serve, optional

The best way to make this is to scrub the potatoes, boil them in
their skins, then slip off the skins with a sharp knife. It can also be

made with left-over cooked potato, or potatoes which have been peeled and boiled in the usual way. Undercook the potatoes so that they are still a bit firm. Cut them into even-sized pieces and mix with the mayonnaise, yogurt and seasoning. This looks pretty served on a base of fresh lettuce leaves with some chopped spring onion sprinkled on top.

9 Green Magic

Vegetables, home-grown, or bought in season, are excellent value for money, as well as being very good for you. They can form the basis of some filling main meals, as well as being indispensable for serving alongside other main courses. Salads, at the end of this section, are equally useful, and they, too, can be main courses in their own right as well as being delicious served with other dishes. They are particularly good value, because a few vegetables go a long way when served raw, and of course, they're packed with vitality, too!

Basic Preparation

The golden rule with vegetables is to trim away as little as possible and cook for as short a time as possible in as little water as possible. Stop cooking the vegetables as soon as they're just tender – they're much nicer like this, as well as being more nutritious. This means cooking sprouts for not more than 3–4 minutes (they're best cut into halves or quarters before cooking), sliced courgettes for about 2 minutes, cabbage and cauliflower florets for about 5 minutes. The exceptions to this rule are root vegetables, which should be just covered with water, but they, too, only need to be boiled until they're just tender – don't let them get anywhere near being soggy!

To microwave

All vegetables cook well in a microwave, requiring the minimum of water and retaining their full colour. Prepare the vegetables as usual and cut into even-sized pieces, not too big. Put these into a shallow wide microwave-proof dish if possible, so that they are spread out. Sprinkle 2–4 tablespoons of water on top, cover with a plate, then microwave on full until the vegetables are tender, stirring once or twice. After cooking let the vegetables stand, still covered, for 5–10 minutes, to continue cooking in their own heat. The timing for the vegetables depends on the size of the pieces, the type of vegetable, and the quantity being cooked, but as a general rule, potatoes or root vegetables take 2–9 minutes for a 4-serving quantity, about 5 minutes for a single serving; cabbage and spinach take about 6 minutes for 4 servings, 3–4 minutes for 1 serving.

COOKER-TOP DISHES
Cabbage and Cashew Nut Stir-Fry

Quick, easy and delicious. Serve this with some hot boiled brown rice. The stir-fry can be ready in minutes, but start cooking the brown rice 30–50 minutes before you want to eat the meal: see page 155. For one serving, use 175–225 g (6–8 oz) prepared cabbage and a quarter of the other ingredients.

Serves 4   320 calories in each serving

700 g (1½ lb) firm white
   cabbage, such as Primo or
   January King
2 tablespoons oil
1 teaspoon turmeric
2 tablespoons desiccated
   coconut

25–50 g (1–2 oz) raisins
100 g (4 oz) broken cashew nuts
salt and freshly ground black
   pepper

Wash the cabbage and shred fairly finely, removing any coarse stems. Just before you want to eat, heat the oil in a large saucepan or wok and put in the cabbage and turmeric. Stir-fry for about 3 minutes, until the cabbage has softened a little, then add the coconut, raisins, cashew nuts and some seasoning. Stir well, then serve.

Sweet and Sour Cabbage and Peanut Stir-Fry

A delicious mixture of sweet and sour flavours with the crunch and nourishment of peanuts. If you are planning to serve this with cooked brown rice (which goes very well with it) get the rice on to cook well in advance, as the stir-fry is very quick to make, and the rice takes 45 minutes. For one person, use half these quantities – you may prefer to use either a green or a red pepper.

Serves 2–4, depending on accompaniments
300–600   calories in each serving

2 tablespoons vegetable oil
125 g (4 oz) raw peanuts
1 red pepper, de-seeded and
   chopped
1 green pepper, de-seeded and
   chopped

1 onion, peeled and chopped
225 g (8 oz) cabbage, shredded
2 celery sticks, chopped
2 large carrots, coarsely grated
   or cut into thin matchsticks

For the sweet and sour dressing

2 garlic cloves, peeled and
  crushed
walnut-sized piece of fresh
  ginger, grated

4 tablespoons soy sauce
4 tablespoons lemon juice
1 tablespoon wine vinegar
2 tablespoons clear honey

First of all make the sweet and sour dressing: put all the ingredients into a small bowl and mix together. Make the stir-fry just before you want to eat: it only takes a few minutes to cook. Fry the peanuts in the oil in a large saucepan or wok for 4–5 minutes, until lightly browned, then add the vegetables and stir-fry for 2 minutes, until they are beginning to soften. Finally pour in the sweet and sour mixture and stir-fry for a further 1–2 minutes to heat through.

Ratatouille

This easy-to-make summer stew is good with cooked brown rice or crusty bread and a crisp salad. If you're serving it with brown rice, get this on to cook (see page 155) before you start making the ratatouille, so that they will be ready together. For two servings, halve all the ingredients; for one, use a medium-sized onion, 1 red pepper, 1 tablespoonful of olive oil, 1 garlic clove, 1 smallish courgette, 1 small aubergine and 2–3 largish tomatoes.

Serves 4   200 calories in each serving

2 large onions, peeled and
  chopped
450 g (1 lb) red peppers,
  de-seeded and sliced
3 tablespoons olive oil
3 garlic cloves, crushed
450 g (1 lb) courgettes or
  marrow, cut into even-sized
  pieces

450 g (1 lb) aubergines, diced
700 g (1½ lb) tomatoes,
  skinned and chopped
salt and freshly ground black
  pepper
chopped parsley

Fry the onions and peppers gently in the oil in a large pan for 5 minutes. Don't let them brown. Then add the garlic, courgettes or marrow and aubergines. Stir, then cover the saucepan and cook for 20–25 minutes, until all the vegetables are tender. Then put in the tomatoes and cook, uncovered, for a further 4–5 minutes, to heat the tomatoes through. Season and sprinkle with chopped parsley.

OVEN-BAKES

Cheese and Aubergine Bake

This is quite economical when aubergines are reasonably priced. It's best when made with Mozzarella cheese, but any cheese can be used. Serve it with a green salad. Use half these quantities and bake for 30–40 minutes for a two person quantity; for one person, use a 225 g (8 oz) aubergine, a medium-sized onion, 1 tablespoonful of oil, a small garlic clove, 2 fresh skinned or canned tomatoes, 40–50g (1½–2 oz) Mozzarella cheese and a tablespoonful of Parmesan, and bake for about 30 minutes.

Serves 4 450 calories in each serving

900 g (2 lb) aubergines
olive or groundnut oil
2 large onions
2 garlic cloves, crushed
425 g (15 oz) can tomatoes
salt and freshly ground black
  pepper

225 g (8 oz) cheese, preferably
  Mozzarella, thinly sliced
2–3 heaped tablespoons grated
  Parmesan cheese

Cut the aubergines into 1 cm (½ inch) dice, sprinkle with salt, place in a colander, put a weight on top and leave for 30 minutes. Then rinse the aubergines under cold water and squeeze as much liquid out of them as you can. Set the oven to 200°C/400°F/Gas Mark 6. Heat a little oil in a large saucepan and fry the onion and garlic for 10 minutes. Then remove from the pan with a draining spoon, and fry the aubergine pieces, until they're crisp and lightly browned, adding more oil if necessary. Drain and blot the aubergines with kitchen paper. Layer the aubergines, onions, tomatoes and cheese into an ovenproof dish, sprinkling some Parmesan cheese and salt and pepper between the layers and ending with a layer of aubergines. Bake, uncovered, for 40–60 minutes.

Root Vegetable Crumble

Make half these quantities for two people and bake for 20–30 minutes; for one person, make a quarter of the amount and bake in an individual ovenproof dish for 15–20 minutes.

Serves 4 450 calories in each serving

1 kg (2 lb 4 oz) prepared,
  cooked root vegetables:
  carrots, swedes, turnips,
  onions

400 ml (¾ pint) bechamel,
  tomato, cheese or mushroom
  sauce, (see page 28)

For the crumble topping

2 heaped tablespoons plain
   100% wholewheat flour
4 heaped tablespoons rolled
   oats
pinch of salt

50 g (2 oz) butter
50 g (2 oz) brazil nuts or hazel
   nuts, chopped
50 g (2 oz) grated cheese

Set the oven to 200°C/400°F/Gas Mark 6. Put the vegetables into a shallow ovenproof dish and pour the sauce over them. To make the crumble, put the flour, oats and salt into a bowl and rub in the butter, until there are no pieces visible, then mix in the nuts and grated cheese. Spoon this mixture evenly over the top of the vegetables and sauce, pressing down lightly. Bake for 30–40 minutes, until the top is crisp and lightly browned.

VARIATION

This crumble topping can be used with any cooked vegetables; it is good on top of cauliflower, courgettes, leeks, spinach, or a ratatouille mixture (see page 88). For a very labour-saving dish, use 450 g (1 lb) skinned and chopped tomatoes and 450 g (1 lb) button mushrooms. Slice and lightly fry the mushrooms, then mix them with the tomatoes and put the crumble on top.

Sweetcorn Bake

Another simple dish to make, using frozen sweetcorn. Use half these quantities for a two-person serving and bake for 20–30 minutes; for one person, use 50 g (2 oz) sweetcorn, 5 tablespoons of milk and 1 egg. Serve this bake with some sliced tomatoes and crusty bread.

Serves 4   320 calories in each serving

25 g (1 oz) butter
300 ml (10 fl oz) milk
4 slices of wholewheat bread,
    crusts removed
225 g (8 oz) frozen sweetcorn
    kernels, thawed (in a sieve
    under the hot tap)

2 eggs
pinch of cayenne pepper or
    chilli powder (optional)
salt and freshly ground black
    pepper
50 g (2 oz) grated cheese

Set the oven to 190°C/375°F/Gas Mark 5. Heat the butter and milk
in a saucepan until the butter has melted, remove from the heat and
crumble in the bread. Leave it on one side while you grease a
shallow ovenproof dish, then mix the bread and milk, breaking up
any large pieces and beat in the rest of the ingredients except for the
cheese. Pour the mixture into the dish, bake for 35–40 minutes,
until set and golden brown.

Cauliflower and Green Pea Terrine

This is a stripy terrine for serving cold with some salad and crusty
bread.

Serves 4   280 calories in each serving

40 g (1½ oz) butter
1 heaped and 1 level tablespoon
    flour
300 ml (½ pint) milk
1 egg
½ small cauliflower, cooked
    and drained

50 g (2 oz) grated cheese
125 g (4 oz) frozen peas
1 tablespoon chopped mint
salt and freshly ground black
    pepper

Set the oven to 170°C/325°F/Gas Mark 3. Line a 450 g (1 lb) loaf
tin with a long strip of greaseproof or non-stick paper to cover the
bottom and narrow sides; grease well. Melt the butter in a saucepan

and stir in the flour; cook for a few seconds until the flour froths, then add the milk. Stir well, over the heat, until the mixture thickens. Let it simmer gently for 10 minutes, then remove from the heat and beat in the egg. Liquidize half the sauce with the cauliflower and cheese; season. Transfer to a bowl. Liquidize the rest of the sauce with the peas and mint; season. Put half the green pea mixture into the base of the loaf tin, level; spoon half the cauliflower mixture on top, then put in the rest of the pea mixture, and finally the rest of the cauliflower mixture. Stand the loaf tin in a roasting tin, half fill the roasting tin with boiling water, and bake for 1 hour, or until the terrine is firm. Leave to get completely cold, then chill. Loosen the sides of the terrine, turn it out, and serve in slices.

Broccoli Roulade with Mushroom Filling

This is much easier to make than it sounds and makes a cheap yet special first course or lunch dish when spinach is in season.

Serves 3–4   310–410 calories in each serving

450 g (1 lb) fresh trimmed broccoli or 450 g (1 lb) frozen broccoli	*salt and freshly ground black pepper*
15 g (½ oz) butter	*4 eggs, separated*
	a little grated Parmesan cheese

For the filling:

175 g (6 oz) button mushrooms	*150 ml (6 fl oz) single cream*
15g (½ oz) butter	*grated nutmeg*
1 teaspoon cornflour	

Cook the fresh broccoli in 1cm (½ inch) boiling water for 6–7 minutes, until the broccoli is tender, then drain thoroughly and liquidize. Cook frozen broccoli according to instructions on the packet, drain well. Add the butter, a little salt and pepper and the egg yolks.

Line a shallow 18 × 28 cm (7 × 11 inch) swiss roll tin with greased greaseproof paper to cover the base of the tin and extend 5 cm (2 inches) up each side. Sprinkle with Parmesan cheese. Set the oven to 200°C/400°F/Gas Mark 6. Whisk the egg whites until stiff but not dry and fold them into the broccoli mixture. Pour the mixture into the prepared tin and bake for 10–15 minutes, until risen and springy to touch.

While the roulade is cooking, make the filling. Heat the butter in a saucepan and fry the mushrooms for 2–3 minutes. Then add the cornflour and cream and stir over the heat until thickened. Season with salt, pepper and grated nutmeg.

Have ready a large piece of greaseproof paper dusted with Parmesan cheese and turn the roulade out on to this; strip off the greaseproof paper from the roulade. Spread the filling over the roulade, then roll it up like a Swiss roll and slide it on to a warmed serving dish. Return to the oven for 5 minutes to heat through. Serve immediately.

SALADS

A substantial salad, such as one based on grated or shredded cabbage or root vegetables, makes an excellent light meal, cheap, healthy and filling. Serve it with some wholewheat bread or a crusty roll (or a hot baked potato) to make it more substantial if you like. A salad like this also makes a great packed lunch for an adult. Transport it in a polythene container and take the roll separately. Don't forget to pack a fork as well. If you make extra, it saves time, and the salad will keep in the fridge for 24 hours.

Vinaigrette Dressing

A quick to make useful basic for all salads. If you make plenty in a jar, it will keep well in the fridge for several days, ready for when you need it. These quantities can be multiplied up.

80–90 calories per tablespoon

1 garlic clove, peeled and crushed
1 teaspoon salt
1 tablespoon made mustard

3 tablespoons red wine vinegar
10 tablespoons best quality olive oil
freshly ground black pepper

Put all the ingredients into a screwtop jar and shake vigorously until blended and quite thick-looking. Check flavouring; more crushed garlic can be added, or more salt. Some chopped herbs are good in it, too, though don't add these if you're planning to keep the dressing in the fridge for over a week.

CABBAGE-BASED SALADS

Firm white (or pale green) cabbages are available all the year round, are always good value, and make an excellent salad base. Wash the cabbage, opening between the layers as well as you can, to remove traces of any chemicals. Then grate the cabbage, or shred it finely with a knife, and leave it in fine shreds, or chop these up into small pieces. If you have a food processor, you can put the cabbage into this in chunks, along with any other ingredients which need chopping, such as carrot and onion, and some dressing, and have your salad ready in moments.

Crunchy Cabbage and Peanut Salad

For one person, make half this quantity.

Serves 2–4   140–280 calories in each serving, without dressing

350 g (12 oz) white cabbage,
  finely shredded
2 large scraped carrots, coarsely
  grated
1 medium-sized red pepper,
  de-seeded and chopped
vinaigrette dressing

2 tablespoons chopped parsley,
  chives or spring onions
  (optional)
2 tablespoons raisins
50 g (2 oz) roasted peanuts

Put all the cabbage into a bowl with the carrots, pepper and enough vinaigrette to moisten it and make it shiny. Then add the other ingredients and mix well. If the salad has to wait before being eaten, save the peanuts to add at the last minute, so that they stay crisp.

Crunchy Cabbage and Apple Salad

Make half this quantity for a main-meal salad for one; if there's some over, it will keep in the fridge for a day.

Serves 2–4   100–150 calories in each serving, without dressing

450 g (1 lb) white cabbage,
  finely shredded
2 apples, cored and diced
2 cooked beetroots, skinned and
  diced

2 celery sticks, chopped
6 spring onions, sliced
vinaigrette dressing to moisten

Put all the salad ingredients into a bowl and mix together.

Coleslaw

Make a third of this quantity for one person, using a small onion and a smallish carrot.

Serves 2–4   180–350 calories in each serving

450 g (1 lb) white cabbage,
   finely shredded
225 g (8 oz) scraped carrots,
   coarsely grated
2 onions, peeled and finely
   chopped
3–4 tablespoons raisins or
   sultanas (optional)

3–4 tablespoons good quality
   mayonnaise, mixed half and
   half with plain yogurt; or just
   plain yogurt, or soured cream
   blended with a teaspoon of
   made mustard
salt and freshly ground black
   pepper

Put all the cabbage, carrot, onion and raisins or sultanas, if you're using them, into a large bowl. Add your chosen dressing and stir in, to make a creamy mixture. Season.

ROOT-BASED SALADS

Root vegetables – carrots, swedes, celeriac and raw beetroot – make good substantial salads. Like cabbage salad, these can make a filling light meal on their own or with some bread or a baked potato. To grate the vegetables, use the coarse side of one of those box graters which you can stand on a board or over a bowl, or use the grating attachment on a food processor.

Crunchy Carrot and Celery Salad

This makes a filling lunch or goes well as an accompaniment to a soft-textured main course such as parsley eggs or cheese soufflé. Make half these quantities for a main-meal salad for one person, a quarter of the quantities if you're serving it alongside something else.

Serves 2–4   25–50 calories in each serving, without dressing

3–4 carrots, coarsely grated
1 good-sized celery heart,
  chopped
1 small green pepper, de-seeded
  and chopped

vinaigrette dressing
salt and freshly ground black
  pepper

Put the carrot, celery and green pepper into a bowl and moisten with a little dressing. Mix well until everything is coated with the dressing. Check seasoning and adjust as necessary.

Carrot, Fennel and Spring Onion Salad

Use 1 large or 2 smaller fennel bulbs instead of the celery, and a bunch of spring onions, finely chopped, instead of the green pepper.

Swede and Date Salad

Make a quarter of these quantities for one person, half for two people.

Serves 4   30 calories in each serving, without dressing

450 g (1 lb) raw swede, peeled
  and grated
4 tablespoons chopped dates
good quality mayonnaise or
  mayonnaise and plain yogurt

salt and freshly ground black
  pepper
a little cress, if available

Put the swede into a bowl with the dates. Add enough mayonnaise or mayonnaise and yogurt, or just yogurt, to make a creamy mixture. Season. Serve sprinkled with cress, if available.

Celeriac Salad

Make a quarter of these quantities for one person, half for two.

Serves 4   20 calories in each serving, without dressing

*450 g (1 lb) celeriac, peeled and
    coarsely grated or cut into
    fine matchsticks*
*vinaigrette dressing or good
    quality mayonnaise or
    mayonnaise and plain yogurt
    or soured cream mixed with
    some made mustard*

*salt and freshly ground black
    pepper*

Put the celeriac into a bowl and add enough of your chosen dressing to moisten. Season.

Raw Beetroot Salad

Serves 4   90 calories in each serving, without dressing

*450 g (1 lb) raw beetroot peeled
    and coarsley grated*
*1 apple, grated, or 1 onion (a
    purple one is nice) cut into
    fine rings*

*4 tablespoons raisins (optional)
vinaigrette dressing*

Put the beetroot into a bowl with the apple or onion and raisins, if you're using them, and add enough vinaigrette to moisten. Season.

TOMATO-BASED SALADS

There's no salad nicer than one made from firm, juicy tomatoes, and when they're in season it can be made quite economically. Tomato salad goes well with many savoury dishes, adding just the right touch of moisture as well as a flash of vivid colour. Or, if you add some little cubes of cheese to a tomato salad, it can become a meal in itself – lovely with some crusty French bread.

Tomato Salad

Allow a large tomato and a few slices of raw onion ring for each person. Wash the tomato and slice it thinly: the tomatoes don't need peeling if they're as good and firm as they should be for this salad. Put the tomato and onion into a shallow dish, sprinkle with a little salt and freshly ground black pepper and a few drops of olive oil. You can add a few drops of wine vinegar just before serving, if you like, but don't put it on too soon, or the tomato juices will run too much. Some chopped fresh basil is the finishing touch to this salad, if you can get it.

Greek Salad

For this delicious, substantial salad, for each person you need; 1–2 large tomatoes, a 5 cm (2 inch) piece of cucumber, a few slices of raw onion, 3 or 4 large juicy black olives, 25–50 g (1–2 oz) white cheese, ideally Feta, but crumbly Lancashire, Cheshire or Wensleydale will do, and a little vinaigrette. Slice the tomatoes, peel and dice the cucumber and mix in a bowl with the onion, olives, cheese and enough vinaigrette just to moisten. Serve with crusty bread.

100

Tomato, Cucumber and Celery Salad

Serves 2–4   36–70 calories in each serving, without dressing

1 head of celery, washed and
  sliced
4 firm tomatoes, sliced

½ cucumber, peeled and sliced
lemon juice or vinaigrette
salt and pepper

Put all the ingredients into a bowl and mix together.

GREEN-BASED SALADS

Green salad is useful for serving with many cooked dishes, particularly many of the quick dishes in this book. It is helpful for the cook in a hurry, because it's much quicker to do than cooking vegetables. You do need crisp, fresh ingredients. Crisp lettuce and/or watercress as a base, to which other ingredients can be added as available; some tender spinach leaves are nice shredded into it, so are a few dandelion leaves or some rocket, which has a hot, spicy flavour. Other fresh herbs can be added as available, and onion or spring onion can be added to taste.

Green Salad

Serves 2–3   20–30 calories in each serving, without dressing

1 lettuce, washed and dried in a
  salad spinner or by patting
  lightly with a clean tea cloth

chopped fresh herbs as available
vinaigrette

Tear the lettuce into bite-sized pieces and put into a bowl with any herbs you may have. Just before you want to serve the salad, spoon a little vinaigrette on to it and turn the salad in this until the leaves are all coated. Serve immediately.

10 Great Stuff

Packing vegetables with a tasty stuffing is a great way to make a few ingredients go a long way and provide a tasty meal, or even one that's a bit special. The stuffing can be made from a cooked rice, breadcrumb, potato or other vegetable base; or it can be made from other tasty vegetables, such as mushrooms, mixed with more concentrated ingredients such as chopped nuts or grated cheese. For extra appeal and nourishment, the vegetables can be served with a well-flavoured sauce.

Stuffed Peppers

This is a light and tasty, but filling, stuffing for peppers and one which can be varied according to vegetables in season. The mushrooms can be replaced by the same quantity of finely diced courgettes or by a 425 g (15 oz) drained can of chick peas. They're good served with a tomato or cheese sauce. For two people, just halve the ingredients, and for one person, just quarter them, using a small onion and 2 teaspoons of oil.

Serves 4   350 calories in each serving

4 green peppers

For the filling:

*1 large onion, peeled and finely
  chopped*
2 tablespoons oil
*225 g (8 oz) mushrooms,
  washed and chopped*
100 g (4 oz) mixed nuts, grated
*100 g (4 oz) tomatoes, skinned
  and chopped*

1 teaspoon mixed dried herbs
1–2 teaspoons yeast extract
*salt and freshly ground black
  pepper*
*4 heaped tablespoons grated
  cheese*

Cut the tops off the green peppers and scoop out the seeds. Wash the peppers, then boil them in 2.5 cm (1 inch) water for 5 minutes, until they are beginning to get tender. Drain them thoroughly, then pat them dry on kitchen paper. Stand them upright in a greased ovenproof dish. Set oven to 180°C/350°F/Gas Mark 4. Fry the onion in the oil for 10 minutes, until tender, then add the mushrooms and cook for a further 2–3 minutes. Remove from the heat and stir in the nuts, herbs, yeast extract and salt and pepper to taste. Spoon this mixture into the peppers, then sprinkle with grated cheese and replace the cut-off tops. Bake for 25–30 minutes.

Stuffed Avocado

A hot stuffed avocado makes an easy and luxurious meal and can be quite economical when avocados are reasonably priced. Serve on a base of cooked rice or creamy mashed potato. Make sure the avocado is really ripe; it should feel slightly soft all over, like a dessert pear does when it's just right for eating. For one person, choose a small avocado and halve the stuffing ingredients.

Serves 2   300 calories in each serving

1 large ripe avocado
lemon juice
1 onion, peeled and chopped
½ green pepper, de-seeded and
*   finely chopped*
15 g (½ oz) butter
1 tomato, skinned and chopped

1 garlic clove, crushed
1 tablespoon chopped parsley
1–2 drops tabasco sauce
salt and freshly ground black
*   pepper*
2 tablespoons grated cheese

Set the oven to 200°C/400°F/Gas Mark 6. Cut the avocado in half, twist the halves in opposite directions and pull apart, then remove the stone. Brush the cut flesh of the avocado with lemon juice. Put the avocado halves into a shallow ovenproof dish. Fry the onion and pepper in the butter for 10 minutes, then remove from the heat and add the tomato, garlic, parsley, tabasco and salt and pepper to taste. Spoon this mixture into the centre of the avocados, sprinkle the grated cheese on top and bake them for 20 minutes, until just heated through. Be careful not to leave them too long, as avocado gets a funny flavour if it's overcooked.

Stuffed Aubergines

Stuffed aubergines make a meal that's a bit special, they're well worth the trouble and work out quite economical when aubergines are reasonably priced. Serve them with creamy mashed potato and a lightly-cooked green vegetable. For one person, halve these quantities, using a small onion.

Serves 2   180 calories in each serving

1 large aubergine or 2 smaller
    ones, about 450 g (1 lb)
    altogether
olive or groundnut oil
1 large onion, peeled and
    chopped
2 tomatoes, skinned and
    chopped

1 tablespoon chopped fresh
    parsley
1–2 garlic cloves, crushed
salt and freshly ground black
    pepper
2 tablespoons soft wholewheat
    breadcrumbs and a little
    butter for topping

Remove the stalk and cut the aubergine or aubergines in half across. Make lots of cuts across the flesh without piercing the skin and sprinkle with salt, putting it in between the cuts. Leave for 30 minutes. Then rinse the aubergines under cold water and squeeze as much liquid out of them as you can. Scoop the flesh out of the skins, chop the flesh. Set the oven to 200°C/400°F/Gas Mark 6. Heat a little oil in a large saucepan and fry the aubergine skins for about 3 minutes on both sides. Remove from the pan, place in a shallow ovenproof dish. Then fry the onion and aubergine flesh for 7 minutes. Add the tomatoes and garlic and fry for a further 3 minutes. Add the parsley, season with salt and pepper. Spoon this mixture into the aubergine skins, sprinkle with the crumbs, dot with butter and bake for 20–30 minutes.

Stuffed Cabbage Rolls

This is a bit fiddly to make, but a great way of creating a filling and interesting meal out of practically nothing. Serve with another cooked vegetable, such as carrots (or a crunchy carrot and celery salad, page 97) and a baked potato. The quantities can easily be quartered or halved if you're making this for one or two people; in this case, reduce the cooking time to 20–30 minutes.

Serves 4   700 calories in each serving

8 outer leaves of cabbage (Savoy,
   Primo or January King)
1 onion, peeled and chopped
2 tablespoons oil
100 g (4 oz) walnuts or roasted
   peanuts, chopped

12 heaped tablespoons soft
   wholewheat breadcrumbs
425 g (15 oz) can tomatoes
salt and freshly ground black
   pepper
300 ml (½ pint) cheese sauce

To finish:

50 g (2 oz) grated cheese

Set the oven to 190°C/375°F/Gas Mark 5. Put the cabbage leaves into
a saucepan of boiling water for 2–3 minutes, to soften them, then
drain well. Fry the onion in the oil for 10 minutes, add the nuts,
breadcrumbs, tomatoes and seasoning. Divide the mixture between
the cabbage leaves, roll them up and place them side by side in a
greased shallow ovenproof dish. Pour the sauce over the cabbage rolls,
sprinkle with the grated cheese and bake for 40–45 minutes, until
golden brown and bubbling.

Tomatoes with Spicy Stuffing

Those big tomatoes – beefsteak tomatoes – make a filling meal when
stuffed with this spicy potato mixture and served with some cooked
rice and a green salad. Halve these ingredients for one person.

Serves 2   300 calories in each serving

2 large beefsteak tomatoes
1 onion, peeled and chopped
2 tablespoons oil
225 g (8 oz) potato, peeled and
   cut into 6 mm (¼) inch dice

1 garlic clove, crushed
1 teaspoon cumin seeds
½ teaspoon turmeric
salt and freshly ground black
   pepper

Cut the tops off the tomatoes, then scoop out the pulp. Chop the pulp, spread it evenly over the base of a lightly greased shallow ovenproof dish that's big enough to hold the two tomatoes. Sprinkle the inside of each tomato with salt, then turn them upside down to drain. Next, make the potato filling. Fry the onion in the oil for 5 minutes, then add the potato and garlic. Cook gently for 10 minutes, then add the spices, and cook for a further 4–5 minutes, until all the potato is just tender. Season. Set the oven to 200°C/400°F/Gas Mark 6. Spoon the potato mixture into the tomatoes. Stand the tomatoes in the dish on top of the tomato pulp, replace their sliced-off tops, and bake for 15–20 minutes, until the tomatoes are just tender.

Tomatoes with Courgette and Corn Stuffing

A colourful and tasty stuffing for large tomatoes – they're good with some softly mashed or pureed potatoes. Halve the ingredients if you're making this for one person.

Serves 2   250 calories in each serving

2 large beefsteak tomatoes
1 onion, peeled and chopped
25 g (1 oz) butter
1 medium-sized courgette, cut
  into 6 mm (¼ inch) dice
125 g (4 oz) fresh sweetcorn,
  scraped off the cob, or frozen
  sweetcorn

1 garlic clove, crushed
salt and freshly ground black
  pepper

Cut the tops off the tomatoes, then scoop out the pulp. Chop the pulp, spread it evenly over the base of a lightly greased shallow ovenproof dish that's big enough to hold the two tomatoes. Sprinkle the inside of each tomato with salt, then turn them upside down to drain. Next, make the filling. Fry the onion in the butter for 5 minutes, then add the courgette, garlic and sweetcorn. Cook gently for 10 minutes, then remove from the heat and season. Set the oven to 200°C/400°F/Gas Mark 6. Spoon the courgette mixture into the tomatoes. Stand the tomatoes in the dish on top of the tomato pulp, replace their sliced-off tops, and bake for 15–20 minutes, until the tomatoes are just tender.

Marrow with Sage and Onion Stuffing

This is good with some apple sauce, roast potatoes and cooked vegetables. To make this for one or two people, use a quarter or half the stuffing ingredients and a large courgette or small marrow.

Serves 4–6   220–320 calories in each serving

*1 medium-sized marrow,
  weighing about 1 kilo (2¼ lb)*
*2 large onions, peeled and
  chopped*
50 g (2 oz) butter
225 g (8 oz) fresh breadcrumbs

*2–3 tablespoons chopped fresh
  sage*
*salt and freshly ground black
  pepper*
a little extra butter
greaseproof paper

Set the oven to 200°C/400°F/Gas Mark 6. Cut the stalk off the marrow, then peel, keeping it whole. Cut a slice off one end, and, using a spoon, scoop out all the seeds, to leave a cavity for stuffing. Fry the onions in the butter for 10 minutes, until soft, then add the breadcrumbs, sage and seasoning. Push the mixture into the marrow, then replace the sliced off end. Grease a large piece of greaseproof paper with butter and wrap the marrow completely in this. Place in a baking tin. Bake for about 1 hour, until the marrow is tender when pierced with a skewer. Remove the greaseproof paper and serve, cut into slices.

11 Easy as Pie

Being able to make good pastry is one of the most useful assets for the busy, budget-conscious cook. It enables you to turn a few bits and pieces into a good meal, at very little expense, and is universally popular and appealing.

I use a wholewheat flour for all pastry; it's healthy and very tasty. Wholewheat pastry is a little difficult to handle, because it is not very elastic, but after one or two goes you soon get used to the feel of it. And if it breaks, you can always patch it together – it will probably taste excellent, if it's that crumbly.

There are various types of wholewheat flour, but basically the difference is that the flour can be milled and packaged just as it is, in which case it's called 100% wholewheat, or it can be sieved a bit, to take out the coarsest bran, and what's left is 85% of the whole grain. Ordinary white flour contains about 72% of the grain. Ideally I like to have a bag of 100% plain flour, a bag of 85% self-raising, which I see one manufacturer is packaging as 'self-raising wholewheat', and a bag of 85% plain, which can usually only be obtained at health shops. These flours will keep for several months in a cool place, and it's useful to have the various types to hand.

As far as fat is concerned, I feel that butter gives the best results, and the 'concentrated butter' which you can sometimes get, is a good buy. The only kind of margarine I would consider using would be a 'high-in-polyunsaturates' one, which, like butter, is expensive, but, from the health point of view, I think good-quality fats (either butter or polyunsaturated margarine) are a worthwhile investment.

One tip, when you're handling any kind of wholewheat pastry, it helps to roll the pastry out on a board, then you can tip it straight from the board into your tin or dish, avoiding any breakages.

Quick Quiche

This is a quick quiche made with a very light pastry which melts in your mouth and doesn't need to be baked blind. If you're cooking for one, this mixture is delicious made into individual size flans using old deepish saucers or 10 cm (8 inch) flan tins or glass dishes. Use half these ingredients to make one flan, or make two and freeze or keep one for later. Bake these flans for about 20 minutes.

Serves 2–4   as a main meal   300–600 calories in each serving, using milk

For the pastry

100 g (4 oz) (4 rounded tablespoons) self-raising 85% wholewheat flour

½ teaspoon salt
65 g (2½ oz) butter or polyunsaturated margarine

For the filling

150 ml (¼ pint) milk, or, for a luxury version, single cream (a 150 ml carton)
2 eggs
2 tablespoons finely chopped onion

2 heaped tablespoons chopped parsley
salt and freshly ground black pepper

110

Set the oven to 190°C/375°F/Gas Mark 5. Put a baking sheet into the centre of the oven, to heat up. Lightly grease a 20 cm (8 inch) flan tin. Put the wholewheat flour into a bowl with the salt and rub in the fat with your fingertips until the mixture looks like fine breadcrumbs. Press the mixture together to make a dough – as the proportion of fat is a little higher than usual, you shouldn't need to add any water. Roll out the pastry and ease into the tin, press down and trim edges. Whisk together the milk or cream and the eggs. Add the parsley and seasoning to taste. Pour the mixture into the flan case. Place the flan case in the oven, on the baking sheet. Bake the flan for 35–40 minutes, until the filling is set and lightly browned. Serve hot, or warm.

Variations

Carrot Quiche: Use 1 large grated carrot instead of, or as well as, the parsley.

Mushroom Quiche: Use 125 g (4 oz) button mushrooms, thinly sliced. Omit or keep the parsley, whichever you prefer.

Spring Onion Quiche: Omit the onion and parsley and use a bunch of spring onions, finely chopped.

Sweetcorn Quiche: Use 125 g (4 oz) frozen sweetcorn kernels instead of the onion and parsley.

Cheese and Tomato Quiche: Omit the parsley and use 50–100 g (2–4 oz) grated cheese and 1 thinly sliced tomato.

Mint and Pea Quiche: Use 2 tablespoons of finely chopped mint instead of the parsley, and 125 g (4 oz) frozen peas. This mixture is good with or without the onion.

Quick Beany Quiche: Add ½ teaspoon made mustard to the eggs and milk and put the well-drained contents of ½ 425 g (15 oz) can butter beans, chick peas or cannellini beans on the pastry before pouring on the milk mixture. If you prefer, leave out the onion and parsley. A crushed garlic clove mixed in with the eggs is also nice in this, and so are a few juicy black olives, depending on how flavourful you like your quiches.

FAST FLANS

In these recipes, the pastry case is baked in the oven while you're preparing the filling.

Basic Pastry Flan Case

This is the basis of the following three recipes. Divide quantities in half to make one smaller flan for one person, using an old, deep saucer, or 10 cm/4 inch flan tin or dish and baking for 10 minutes.

Makes one 20 cm (8 inch) flan case or two 10 cm (4 inch) flan cases

830 calories, for whole amount

100 g (4 oz) (4 rounded tablespoons) plain wholewheat flour, 100% or 85%

pinch of salt
50 g (2 oz) butter
6 teaspoons cold water

Set the oven to 200°C/400°F/Gas Mark 6. Put a baking sheet into the centre of the oven, to heat up. Lightly grease a 20 cm (8 inch) flan tin. Sift the flour into a large bowl, adding the residue of bran from the sieve if you're using 100% flour. Add the salt, then rub in the butter until the mixture looks like fine breadcrumbs. Mix to a dough with the water. Roll out the pastry and ease it into the tin. Press down, trim the edges. Put the flan into the oven to bake for 10 minutes while you're preparing the filling.

Poverty Pie

A friend gave me this recipe for what in her family is referred to as 'poverty pie' – an end of the week dish to put together from storecupboard ingredients and oddments from the fridge. To make this for one person, halve all the ingredients except for the egg. Bake for 15–20 minutes.

Serves 4   420–480 calories in each serving

Pastry flan case made as described above

For the filling

25 g (1 oz) butter
1 rounded tablespoon flour
300 ml (½ pint) milk
50 g –100 g (2–4 oz) grated
  cheese

1 egg, separated
½ teaspoon made mustard
salt and freshly ground black
  pepper

Set the oven to 200°C/400°F/Gas Mark 6. Bake the pastry flan case for 10 minutes, as described above.

While the flan case is cooking, make the filling. Put the butter, flour and milk into a saucepan and whisk over a moderate heat until thickened. Remove from the heat and add most of the cheese, the egg yolk, mustard and salt and pepper to taste. Whisk the egg white until stiff then fold into the mixture. Pour the mixture into the flan case, sprinkle with the rest of the cheese and put into the oven. Turn the heat down to 190°C/375°F/Gas Mark 5. Bake for 20 minutes, until puffed up and golden brown.

Mixed Vegetable Flan

You can use left-over cooked vegetables for this, or the mixture of cauliflower and frozen mixed vegetables given in the recipe.

Serves 4 as a main course   420 calories in each serving

For the shortcrust pastry

Wholewheat shortcrust pastry made with 100g flour (see page 112).

For the filling

1 small cauliflower or ½ larger one, washed and broken into even-sized small florets – cut larger ones, if necessary
300 g (10 oz) frozen mixed vegetables

300 g (½ pint) cheese sauce (see page 28)
2 tablespoons grated cheese

Set the oven to 200°C/400°F/Gas Mark 6. Put a baking sheet into the centre of the oven, to heat up. Lightly grease a 20 cm (8 inch) flan tin. Roll out the pastry and ease it into the tin. Press down, trim the edges. Put the flan into the oven to bake for 10 minutes while you're preparing the filling. Put 1 cm (½ inch) water into a medium-sized saucepan and bring to boil, then add the cauliflower and mixed vegetables and boil for 4–5 minutes, until the cauliflower is just tender. Drain well. Add these vegetables to the cheese sauce. Season. Spoon the mixture into the flan case, sprinkle with grated cheese, and pop the flan back into the oven for 15 minutes or so, just to heat through and brown the top. Serve hot.

Sweetcorn Soufflé Flan

A quick and easy flan which is a bit different. The filling rises, and there is quite a generous amount, so if you're cooking for one or two people, use this quantity of pastry to make two 10 cm (4 inch) flan cases, then use 1 egg and half all the other filling ingredients. Bake for about 15 minutes.

Serves 4   430–490 calories in each serving

Pastry flan case made as described above

For the filling

25 g (1 oz) butter
1 rounded tablespoon flour
300 ml (½ pint) milk
100 g (4 oz) frozen sweetcorn
  kernels
50 g–100g (2–4 oz) grated
  cheese

1 egg, separated
½ teaspoon made mustard
salt and freshly ground black
  pepper

Set the oven to 200°C/400°F/Gas Mark 6. Put a baking sheet into the centre of the oven, to heat up. Lightly grease a 20 cm (8 inch) flan tin. Roll out the pastry and ease it into the tin. Press down, trim the edges. Put the flan into the oven to bake for 10 minutes while you're preparing the filling. Put the butter, flour and milk into a saucepan and whisk over a moderate heat until thickened. Remove from the heat and add the sweetcorn, straight from the packet, most of the cheese, the egg yolk, mustard and salt and pepper to taste. Whisk the egg white until stiff then fold into the mixture. Pour the mixture into the flan case, sprinkle with the rest of the cheese and put into the oven. Turn the heat down to 190°C/375°F/Gas Mark 5. Bake for 30 minutes, until puffed up and golden brown.

Mushroom Flan

This flan is a good one to make when mushrooms are cheap, which they sometimes are after a bank holiday, or if you have some field mushrooms. These quantities make a lovely big shallow flan, using a tin measuring 30 cm (12 inches) across; alternatively, you could use two 20 cm (8 inch) tins, or halve the ingredients, if you prefer. For two people, halve the ingredients and use a 20 cm (8 inch) flan tin, and for one person, use a quarter of the quantities (2–3 table-spoons soured cream) and a 5 cm (4 inch) flan tin.

Serves 6 as a main course   380 calories in each serving

Wholewheat shortcrust pastry made with 200g flour (see page 112).

For the filling

1 onion, peeled and chopped	*150 ml (5 fl oz) carton soured*
25 g (1 oz) butter	*cream*
450 g (1 lb) button mushrooms,	*salt, freshly ground black*
washed and sliced	*pepper and nutmeg*
1–2 garlic cloves, crushed	*chopped parsley*
1 teaspoon cornflour	

Set the oven to 200°C/400°F/Gas Mark 6. Put a baking sheet into the centre of the oven, to heat up. Lightly grease a 30 cm (12 inch) flan tin. Roll out the pastry and ease it into the tin. Press down, trim the edges. Put the flan into the oven to bake for 10–15 minutes while you're preparing the filling.

To make the filling, fry the onion in the butter for 10 minutes, then add the mushrooms and garlic and cook for a further 3–4 minutes. Stir in the cornflour and the soured cream; cook for a moment or two until thickened. Then remove from the heat and season with salt, pepper and nutmeg.

Spoon the mushroom filling into the flan case; return the flan to the oven for 10–15 minutes to heat through. Serve hot.

PIES AND PASTIES
Cheese and Onion Pie

This is the basis of the following three recipes. Divide quantities in half to make one smaller pie for two people, or use a quarter of these quantities for one person, using an old, deep heatproof saucer, or small ovenproof dish and baking for 20 minutes.

Serves 4   450–680 calories in each serving

200 g (8 oz) (8 rounded tablespoons) plain wholewheat flour, 100% or 85%

pinch of salt
100 g (4 oz) butter
3 tablespoons cold water

For the filling

3 large onions, sliced
150 g (6 oz) grated cheese

salt and freshly ground black pepper, grated nutmeg

Set the oven to 220°C/425°F/Gas Mark 7. Put a baking sheet into the centre of the oven, to heat up. Sift the flour into a large bowl, adding the residue of bran from the sieve if you're using 100% flour. Add the salt, then rub in the butter until the mixture looks like fine breadcrumbs. Mix to a dough with the water. Set aside to chill while you prepare the filling. Cook the onions in 2.5 cm (1 inch) boiling, salted water for 5 minutes, to soften slightly. Drain and cool. Roll out half the pastry to fit a 20–22 cm (8–9 inch) pie plate. Mix the cheese with the onions and season to taste. Spoon onion mixture on top of the pastry. Roll out the remaining pastry to fit top; press edges together and trim. Bake for 30 minutes.

Variations

Butter Bean, Cheese and Pickle Pie

Make this in the same way, using 125 g (4 oz) butter beans, soaked, cooked and drained, or a 425 g (15 oz) can, drained, in place of one of the onions, and reducing the amount of cheese to 50 g (2 oz). Add 2 heaped tablespoons pickle or chutney to the mixture before spooning on top of the pastry.

Cabbage Pie

This is much more tasty than it sounds, and very good with a sauce made by mixing some chopped fresh herbs (especially fennel or dill) into a small carton of soured cream or plain yogurt. Fry a chopped onion and 450 g (1 lb) shredded white cabbage in 25 g (1 oz) butter until they are tender – 10 minutes – then add 3–4 tablespoons chopped parsley, 75–100 g (3–4 oz) chopped button mushrooms, 2 skinned and chopped tomatoes, 1 teaspoon dried dill weed or caraway seeds, and some salt and freshly ground black pepper to taste. You can also add a couple of chopped hardboiled eggs to this mixture, if you like.

Root Vegetable Pie with Cheesy Pastry

Add 125 g (4 oz) grated cheese to the pastry after you have rubbed in the fat and before you add the water. To make the filling, fry a chopped onion and 2 chopped celery sticks in 25 g (1 oz) of butter for 10 minutes, then add 225 g (8 oz) scraped and chopped carrots, 225 g (8 oz) peeled and diced swede and 225 g (8 oz) peeled and diced turnips or parsnips and 150 ml (¼ pint) water. Cook gently, with a lid on the pan, for about 15 minutes, until the vegetables are just tender. Season and cool. Assemble and cook the pie as described above.

Mushroom and Chestnut Pie

Fry 1 large chopped onion and 2 chopped celery sticks in 25 g (1 oz) of butter for 10 minutes, then add 225 (8 oz) washed and sliced mushrooms and cook for a further 2–3 minutes, or until the mushrooms are tender. Remove from the heat and add 350–450 g (12 oz–1 lb) cooked chestnuts (you can use fresh cooked chestnuts or canned whole chestnuts, or dried ones which have been soaked and cooked as described on page 129). Add a tablespoonful of soy sauce and salt and pepper to taste.

Leek Pie

Wash 900 g (2 lb) leeks and cut them into pieces about 2 cm (1 inch) long. Cook them in 1 cm (½ inch) of boiling water for about 10 minutes, until just tender. Drain them very well, then mix them with 300 ml (½ pint) soured cream or bechamel sauce (see page 27). Season carefully.

Potato and Mushroom Pasties

These quantities can easily be quartered or halved for one or two people.

Makes 4   540 calories in each serving

*200 g (8 oz) (8 rounded
    tablespoons) plain wholemeal
    flour, 100% or 85%*

*½ teaspoonful salt
100 g (4 oz) butter
3 tablespoons water*

For the filling

1 onion, peeled and chopped
2 tablespoons oil
225 g (8 oz) potato, peeled and
  cut into 6 mm (¼ inch) dice
1 garlic clove, crushed

225 g (8 oz) mushrooms,
  washed and chopped
salt and freshly ground black
  pepper

First make the filling. Fry the onion in the oil for 5 minutes, then add the potato and garlic. Cook gently for 10 minutes, until all the vegetables are just tender. Season with salt and pepper. Leave to cool. Set the oven to 200°C/400°F/Gas Mark 6. Next make the pastry as described on page 112 and divide into four pieces; roll each into a circle 15 cm (6 inches) across. Spoon a quarter of the potato mixture on to each, fold up the pastry into a pasty shape and press the edges together. Make a couple of small steam-holes in each pasty, then place the pasties on a baking tray and bake for 20–25 minutes.

Steamed Vegetable Pudding

Other combinations of vegetables can be used for this, depending on what's available. A half quantity can be made in a small bowl and steamed for 1 hour, for two people; or a quarter quantity can be made in a deepish ramekin or old cup for one person, using 50 g (2 oz) flour, 25 g (1 oz) butter and 2–3 teaspoons of water for the pastry and a quarter of the filling ingredients. Steam this for 45 minutes.

Serves 4   400 calories in each serving

175 g (6 oz) (6 rounded
  tablespoons) self-raising
  wholewheat flour 80% or
  100%

½ teaspoon salt
75 g (3 oz) butter or margarine
2–3 tablespoons water

For the filling

1 onion, peeled and chopped	225 g (8 oz) mushrooms, sliced
2 potatoes, peeled and cut into 1 cm (½ inch) dice	2 tablespoons soy sauce
2 carrots, scraped and sliced	salt and freshly ground black pepper

Parboil the vegetables (except the mushrooms) for 10 minutes; drain. Grease a medium-sized 900 ml (1½ pint) pudding basin thoroughly with butter or margarine. Put the flour into a bowl with the salt, then add the butter and rub in with your fingertips. Add enough water to make a dough. Turn this out onto a floured board and knead lightly, then roll out two thirds to fit the pudding basin, press down well. Put in the vegetables, mushrooms, soy sauce and seasoning. Roll out the other piece of dough to fit the top of the pudding, and press down firmly; trim the edges. Prick the top several times with a fork, then cover with a piece of greaseproof paper and a piece of foil and tie down. Stand the basin in a large saucepan with enough water to come half way up the sides of the basin, and simmer gently for 1½ hours. Keep the water level topped up with boiling water from the kettle while the pudding is steaming. To serve the pudding, remove the paper coverings, slip a palette knife around the sides of the basin to loosen the pudding, then turn it out onto a warmed plate. Serve with lightly cooked vegetables or a salad.

PIZZAS

Although there are many ready-to-cook pizzas available now, homemade ones taste better, and this scone-based one is very easy to make. I've included a recipe for a simple yeast-based one, too, because although it takes a bit longer, it's fun to do when you're in the mood.

Quick Pizza

Serves 4–6   330–500 calories in each serving

225 g (8 oz) (8 rounded
   tablespoons) self-raising 85%
   wholewheat flour
½ teaspoon dry mustard
½ teaspoon salt

2 teaspoons baking powder
50 g (2 oz) butter
40 g (1½ oz) grated cheese
150 ml (¼ pint) milk and water

For the topping

2 onions, peeled and chopped
2 tablespoons oil
2 tablespoons tomato puree
50 g (2 oz) button mushrooms
1 small green pepper, de-seeded
   and sliced

50 g (2 oz) grated cheese
2 teaspoons oregano
salt and freshly ground black
   pepper

Set the oven to 220°C/425°F/Gas Mark 7. Sift the flour, mustard powder and baking powder into a bowl, then add the butter and rub in with your fingertips. Add the milk mixture and the grated cheese and mix to a soft but not sticky dough. Turn this out onto a floured board and knead lightly, then roll dough out to fit a large baking sheet or round pizza dish. Prick dough all over. Pop this into the oven for 10 minutes while you prepare the topping. To do this, first fry the onions in the oil for 10 minutes, then add the tomato puree and salt and pepper to taste. Spread this over the pizza base, then put the sliced mushrooms and pepper on top. Sprinkle with the grated cheese and oregano. Put the pizza back into the oven and bake for 20–25 minutes, until puffed up and golden brown on top. A crisp green salad goes well with this.

Yeast Pizza

This proper yeast pizza is easy to do if you take it in stages.

Serves 4–6   500–750 calories in each serving

450 g (1 lb) plain 85%
  wholewheat flour
1 packet instant dried yeast

½ teaspoon salt
about 175 ml (6 fl oz) warm
  water
2 tablespoons oil

For the topping

2 large onions, peeled and
  chopped
oil
4 tablespoons tomato puree
1 garlic clove, crushed
125 g (4 oz) mushrooms,
  washed and sliced or 1 green
  pepper, de-seeded and sliced

125 g (4 oz) sliced cheese,
  Mozzarella preferably, but
  any cheese will do
a few black olives (optional)
oregano
salt and freshly ground black
  pepper

First make the dough. Put the flour, yeast, salt, water and oil into a bowl and mix to a dough. It should be the consistency of well-worked Plasticine. Turn the dough out onto a lightly-floured working surface and continue to knead, stretch and pummel it with your hands for 5 minutes. You will find that it becomes smooth and silky. Put the dough into a bowl, cover with a damp cloth and leave until the dough has doubled in size. This takes about 1 hour in a warm place, or up to 3 hours at room temperature. Then punch down the dough, divide it between two well-greased flan tins or one larger one, or press it into a large circle shape on a baking tray. Put it into a warm place while you make the filling.

Fry the onion in 2 tablespoons of oil for 10 minutes, then add the tomato puree and garlic and season. Set the oven to 250°C/500°F/Gas Mark 9.

Flatten the dough with your hands, pressing it well into the tins and up the sides a little. Spread the tomato mixture on top of the dough, then put the mushrooms or green pepper, the slices of cheese and olives, on top. Drizzle a little oil over the top and sprinkle with oregano. Bake the pizzas for 15–20 minutes, until puffed up and golden brown on top.

12 Nuts!

Nuts feature in recipes in a number of other sections of this book. They are a useful food, because although they sound expensive — and are, if used in large quantities — a little goes a long way, and a dish such as nut burgers, or nut roast, can be surprisingly economical, as well as healthy and good to eat.

You can buy ready-chopped mixed nuts at health shops and some supermarkets (make sure the supermarket ones aren't sweetened) and these are convenient and reasonably-priced. Generally I prefer to buy individual varieties and make my own mixture, and you can usually buy nuts in small quantities, to make this possible on a budget. It's best, anyway, only to buy what you can use within a couple of weeks or so, and to buy from a shop which has a quick turnover, because nuts can go rancid (and not good for you) if kept for too long. Take special care when buying walnuts: if they taste bitter, they're old, and will spoil the flavour of your dish.

Peanuts are cheap and nourishing, but I find you can get tired of them quite quickly and their flavour seems to dominate other nuts, so use carefully. You can buy them in various forms. If you buy the unroasted ones, they are easy to roast at home, and when they're roasted, the skins will just rub off. The same applies to hazelnuts bought with their brown skins still on.

To roast peanuts or hazelnuts: Spread the nuts out on a baking tray and bake in a moderate oven for about 20 mintues, or under a hot grill for about 10 minutes, until the skins will rub off easily and the nuts underneath are brown. Rub off the skins in a soft cloth.

BASIC NUT MIXTURE

Easy Nut Burgers

These don't taste like meat ones, but they have a distinctive flavour and chewy texture of their own. They make a good supper dish, served in soft baps with some sliced tomato and onion. This recipe can easily be multiplied up to serve more people, or halved for one person.

Serves 2–4   400–800 calories in each serving

1 onion, peeled and chopped
1 small celery stick, finely
   chopped
25 g (1 oz) butter
1/2 teaspoon mixed herbs
1 1/2 teaspoons flour
5 tablespoons water
1/2 teaspoon vegetarian stock
   powder
100 g (4 oz) mixed nuts:
   almonds, brazil nuts,
   walnuts, cashew nuts, finely
   chopped or grated

6 heaped tablespoons soft
   wholewheat breadcrumbs
1 1/2 teaspoons soy sauce
1/2 teaspoon yeast extract
salt and freshly ground black
   pepper

To finish

dried breadcrumbs to coat
oil for shallow frying

Fry the onions and celery in the butter for 10 minutes, browning them lightly. Add the herbs, stir for a minute, then mix in the flour and cook for 1–2 minutes. Pour in the water and stir until thickened. Add the stock powder, soy sauce, yeast extract, nuts, breadcrumbs and salt and pepper to taste. Cool, then form into 4 flat burgers about 1 cm (½ inch) thick, and coat with dried breadcrumbs. Pour a little oil into a frying pan, just enough to cover the base thinly, heat, then put in the burgers and fry them until crisp. Turn them over and fry the second side, then drain them on kitchen paper.

Quick Nut Roast

This is good hot, with a mushroom sauce, or cold with salad and some pickles or chutney. Simply quarter or halve the ingredients to make the right quantity for one or two people and bake in a small dish for 15–20 minutes for a one-person size, or 20–30 minutes for a two-person roast.

Serves 4   500 calories in each serving

25 g (1 oz) butter	*2 tomatoes, skinned and chopped*
2 large onions, peeled and finely chopped	*2 tablespoons chopped fresh parsley*
100 g (4 oz) cashew nuts, grated	*1 teaspoon mixed herbs*
100 g (4 oz) hazelnuts or almonds, grated	*2 tablespoons lemon juice*
12 heaped tablespoons soft wholewheat breadcrumbs	*salt and freshly ground black pepper*

Set the oven to 200°C/400°F/Gas Mark 6. Grease a 20 cm (8 inch) square tin or shallow casserole dish. Melt the butter in a large saucepan and fry the onions gently for 10 minutes, until tender. Then add the nuts, breadcrumbs, tomatoes, parsley, mixed herbs, lemon juice and salt and pepper to taste. Press into the prepared tin or casserole dish, smooth top. Bake for 35–40 minutes. Ease the nut roast out of the tin or casserole, cut into wedges and serve.

Easy Carrot and Hazelnut Roast

This is extremely quick to make if you've got a food processor, just put everything into it – the carrot and bread cut into chunks – and whizz until smooth. Even without a food processor, this roast is quickly put together and is moist and tasty to eat. I like it best with a salad, but it's also nice with cooked vegetables. I suggest making a half-quantity of this mixture for one person, and serving the roast once hot, and once cold, with some chutney or a sauce made by mixing plain yogurt with a little real mayonnaise or some chopped spring onions or herbs.

Serves 4 generously 340 calories in each serving

1 large onion, peeled and finely
   chopped
4 medium-sized carrots, scraped
   and grated
6 heaped tablespoons
   wholewheat breadcrumbs
225 g (8 oz) hazelnuts, buy ready
   skinned ones, or buy them in
   their skins and roast as
   described on page 126

2 teaspoons mixed herbs
2 eggs
1 tablespoon soy sauce
salt and freshly ground black
   pepper

Set the oven to 190°C/375°F/Gas Mark 5. Line a 900 g (2 lb) loaf tin or deep casserole dish with a long strip of non-stick or greaseproof paper to cover the base and go up the narrow sides. Grease well. Mix all the ingredients together. Spoon the mixture into the loaf tin or dish and bake for 45–60 minutes, until firm in the middle and lightly browned. Turn the nut roast out of the container, ease off the paper, and serve the roast in thick slices.

Variations

For a more strongly flavoured roast, add 1–2 crushed garlic cloves and perhaps 1–2 teaspoons of yeast extract; a little chopped celery or a pinch or two of celery salt are good in it, too. Or try a curried version: add 2–4 teaspoons of curry powder to the basic mixture. Adding some grated raw ginger – 1–2 tablespoons – is another tasty variation, and so is some chopped rosemary – 1–2 teaspoons. A mushroomy version is good, too; just add 125–225 g (4–8 oz) chopped mushrooms to the basic mixture. There are lots of possibilities, so enjoy experimenting!

CHESTNUTS

Chestnuts are a cheap and useful food – free, if you pick them up in the woods – their only disadvantage being the rather tedious business of skinning them, which doesn't make them labour-saving. If you feel in the mood for doing them – which is quite fun if there's someone to help you and chat with at the same time – here are two good recipes for using them.

How to skin chestnuts: Make a slit in the skin of each chestnut, then either put them into a moderate oven for 10–15 minutes, pop them into a microwave for about 5 minutes, or boil them in water for 10–15 minutes, until the slits open and you can slip off the skins using a sharp knife and holding the chestnuts in a cloth. The chestnuts will probably be quite soft and 'floury' by this time; if they still seem rather raw, just cover them with a little water and simmer them for about 10 minutes, until soft, then drain.

You can buy dried chestnuts at health shops and delicatessens. These are more expensive, of course, but easier. Just soak them for several hours, then simmer them gently until very tender. This may take a couple of hours, depending on how hard the chestnuts are. A pressure cooker is useful for them.

Chestnut Roast

Make half this quantity for two people, and bake for 30–40 minutes; for one, use a quarter of these quantities, and bake for 20–30 minutes.

Serves 4–6   320–470 calories in each serving

900 g (2 lbs) chestnuts – to
   make about 750 g (1½ lb)
   after skinning, or about 250 g
   (8 oz) dried chestnuts
25 g (1 oz) butter
1 large onion, peeled and
   chopped
2 sticks celery, finely chopped
2 tablespoons chopped parsley
2 tablespoons lemon juice
1 garlic clove, crushed
salt and freshly ground black
   pepper
crisp crumbs for coating

Melt the butter and fry the onion and celery for 10 minutes, but don't brown them; remove from the heat and add the chestnuts. Mash well, then mix in the parsley, lemon juice and garlic. Season with salt and pepper. Set the oven to 200°C/400°F/Gas Mark 6. Put a little oil onto the baking tray and put into the oven to heat. Form the chestnut mixture into a roll and coat with the dried crumbs. Put the chestnut roll onto the baking tray and carefully turn it so that it is coated with hot oil. Bake for 45 minutes, until crisp on the outside, spooning a little of the oil over it from time to time.

Chestnut Casserole

Another warming late autumn dish, and a delicious way to use any chestnuts you may find. Some cider or wine, replacing some of the stock, makes this casserole even better. Some cooked Brussels sprouts go well with this and perhaps a baked potato.

Nuts!

Serves 4   500 calories in each serving

25 g (1 oz) butter
1 onion, peeled and chopped
outside sticks from 1 head of
  celery, sliced
1 garlic clove, crushed
225 g (8 oz) mushrooms,
  washed and sliced
900 g (2 lbs) chestnuts, skinned,
  to make about 750 g (1½ lb),
  or 225 g (8 oz) dried
  chestnuts

2 tablespoons flour
225 g (8 oz) can tomatoes
600 g (1 pint) stock
salt and freshly ground black
  pepper

Set oven to 180°C/350°F/Gas Mark 4. Melt the butter and fry the onion and celery for 10 minutes, but don't brown them; add the garlic, mushrooms, and chestnuts and cook for 2–3 minutes. Stir in the flour, then add the tomatoes and stock. Bring up to the boil, then season and transfer to a heatproof casserole and bake for 45–60 minutes. Check seasoning, and serve.

13 Lovely Lentils

Lentils are a useful pulse because not only are they cheap and tasty, they can also be cooked without soaking, so you don't have to think too far ahead. There are two types of lentils which I think taste good. These are the big greeny brown whole lentils which you can get at health shops. They're sometimes called 'green lentils' or may be called 'continental lentils'. There's also a whole brown lentil which is smaller and darker brown. These taste delicious, but I've found that there are often hard pieces of stone mixed in with them, so unless you're prepared to spend time sorting carefully through these lentils, I don't think they are a very good buy. To cook the continental lentils, put them into a saucepan and cover with plenty of cold water – their height again – then bring to the boil, and simmer gently, uncovered, for about 45 minutes, until tender.

The other useful lentils are the split orange ones which you can buy at any supermarket, as well as in health shops. These cook in only 20 minutes. Put them into a saucepan with a double quantity of water – that is, 1 cup of lentils to 2 cups of water – bring to the boil, then cover and cook very gently for 20 minutes, until the lentils are tender and all the water absorbed. Make sure the heat is low, or the lentils will catch. You can use more water and drain off the excess, but if you're making burgers or a roast from the lentils, it's best to have them cooked fairly dry, otherwise you seem to need lots of breadcrumbs to make the mixture shapeable.

SPLIT ORANGE LENTILS

Lentil Roast

Very easy, and delicious served in thick slices with a tasty sauce such as vegetarian gravy or tomato sauce. Mint sauce and some roast potatoes are good with it, too. To make a roast for one or two people, use 1 egg and half of all the other ingredients and bake for about 30 minutes.

Serves 4   460 calories in each serving

225 g (8 oz) split red lentils
400 ml (16 fl oz) water
1 onion, peeled and finely
*   chopped*
25 g (1 oz) butter or margarine
1 teaspoon mixed herbs
125 g (4 oz) grated cheese

1 tablespoon lemon juice
1 egg, beaten
soft wholewheat breadcrumbs
salt and freshly ground black
*   pepper*
wholewheat flour to coat, a
*   little oil for cooking*

Put the lentils and water into a medium-sized saucepan and simmer very gently, uncovered, until the lentils are tender and all the liquid absorbed: about 20 minutes. Set the oven to 190°C/375°F/Gas Mark 5. Fry the onion in the butter for 10 minutes until soft and lightly browned, then add this to the lentils together with the mixed herbs, cheese, lemon juice and beaten egg. Add a few breadcrumbs or crumbled Weetabix to stiffen the mixture if necessary. Turn the mixture out onto a board, coat with wholewheat flour and form into a smooth roll shape. Heat a little oil in a tin in the oven; put in the lentil roll and spoon some of the oil over it. Bake for 45 minutes until browned and crisp, basting with oil from time to time.

Spicy Lentil Burgers

Light, delicious and spicy, these are good with either a salad or cooked vegetables. Some hot boiled rice, or spiced rice goes well with these, and some mango chutney or lime pickle, too. Use a quarter or half of these quantities if you're cooking for one or two people.

Serves 4   400 calories in each serving

350 g (12 oz) split red lentils
750 ml (1¼ pints) water
1 large onion, peeled and finely
  chopped
1 green pepper, de-seeded and
  finely chopped
25 g (1 oz) butter or margarine

1 garlic clove, crushed
1 tablespoon grated fresh ginger
½ teaspoon chilli powder
2 tablespoons chopped parsley
1 tablespoon lemon juice
salt and freshly ground black
  pepper

To coat:

1 egg, beaten with 1 tablespoon
  water

dried breadcrumbs
oil for shallow frying

Put the lentils and water into a medium-sized saucepan and simmer very gently, uncovered, until the lentils are tender and all the liquid absorbed: about 20 minutes. Fry the onion and green pepper in the butter for 10 minutes until soft, then add the garlic and ginger and cook for a minute or two longer. Add this mixture to the lentils together with the chilli powder, lemon juice and parsley. Season carefully. Form into burger shapes, dip in beaten egg, then into breadcrumbs. Pour enough oil into a frying pan to coat the base and set over a moderate heat. When it's hot, put in the burgers and fry until crisp and brown on one side; turn them over with a palette knife and cook the other side. Drain on kitchen paper.

Lentil Dal

This is an easy, spicy mixture that goes well with some plain boiled rice and/or some wedges of hardboiled egg. I rather like it with some sliced tomato and watercress or the spiced tomatoes on page 106; it depends how hungry you're feeling! You can buy coconut cream at health shops, supermarkets and Indian shops. It keeps for months in the fridge. To make enough for two people halve these ingredients; for one person, use a quarter of these quantities. The cooking time is the same as that given.

Serves 4   350 calories in each serving

*1 onion, peeled and finely
   chopped*
15 g (½ oz) butter
1 garlic clove, crushed
250 g (9 oz) split red lentils

½ teaspoon chilli powder
*1 teaspoon each ground cumin,
   turmeric and salt*
750 ml (1¼ pints) water
50 g (2 oz) creamed coconut

Fry the onion in the butter for 10 minutes until soft and lightly browned, then add the garlic, lentils, spices and salt and stir for 2–3 minutes. Add the water, bring to the boil, and simmer gently for 25–30 minutes, until the lentils are tender. Add the creamed coconut and stir over the heat until dissolved. Check the seasoning and serve.

Lentils and Mushrooms Au Gratin

In this recipe, the lentils are made into a thick sauce which is poured over mushrooms, topped with crumbs and grated cheese and baked until crisp and golden brown. Make a half quantity for two people, or a quarter-quantity for one person, baking for 30 minutes or 15 minutes, respectively.

Serves 4   370 calories in each serving

175 g (6 oz) split red lentils	*1 teaspoon yeast extract*
600 ml (1 pint) milk and water mixed	*125 g (4 oz) mushrooms, washed and sliced*
50 g (2 oz) butter or margarine	*4 heaped tablespoons fresh breadcrumbs*
1 large onion, peeled and finely chopped	*4 tablespoons grated cheese*
juice and rind of ½ lemon	
salt and freshly ground black pepper	

Put the lentils and milk-and-water into a medium-sized saucepan and simmer very gently, uncovered, until the lentils are tender and all the liquid absorbed – about 20 minutes. Set the oven to 180°C/350°F/Gas Mark 4. Meanwhile, melt half the butter and fry the onion for 10 minutes until soft and lightly browned, then add this to the lentils together with the lemon juice and rind, salt, pepper and yeast extract; liquidize, sieve, or beat well with a wooden spoon, to make a thick puree. Fry the mushrooms in the rest of the butter for 2–3 minutes, then put them into a shallow ovenproof dish and pour the lentil mixture on top. Sprinkle with breadcrumbs and grated cheese. Bake for 40–45 minutes, until golden and crisp on top, hot and bubbly underneath.

GREEN LENTILS

Lentils with Tomatoes and Thyme

This simple dish is nicest when made with fresh tomatoes, although you could use a 425 g (15 oz) can instead. Serve with crusty rolls. If there's any over, it's very pleasant cold, as a salad. To make enough for fewer people, halve the ingredients for two, quarter them for one.

Serves 4   360 calories in each serving

225 g (8 oz) green lentils
water
25 g (1 oz) butter
2 large onions, peeled and thinly
  sliced
1 garlic clove, crushed
2–3 teaspoons dried thyme

450 g (1 lb) tomatoes, skinned
  and chopped
salt and freshly ground black
  pepper
2–3 tablespoons chopped fresh
  parsley

Put the lentils into a large saucepan with the water and boil gently until tender, about 45 minutes. Drain. Meanwhile melt the butter in a large saucepan and fry the onion until tender. Add the garlic, thyme, tomatoes, drained lentils and parsley. Season with salt and pepper. Re-heat gently, and serve.

Lentil Shepherd's Pie

This can be prepared in advance, ready for cooking, and only needs a quickly-cooked vegetable, such as sprouts or carrots, to go with it. Make a half quantity for two people, and bake for 30 minutes, or a quarter of the amount for one person and bake for 15–20 minutes.

Serves 4   500 calories in each serving

225 g (8 oz) green lentils
water
25 g (1 oz) butter
2 large onions, peeled and thinly
    sliced
1 garlic clove, crushed
1 teaspoon mixed herbs

425 g (15 oz) can tomatoes,
    skinned and chopped
salt and freshly ground black
    pepper
2–3 tablespoons chopped fresh
    parsley

For the topping

750 g (1½ lb) potatoes, peeled
    and cut into even-sized pieces
25 g (1 oz) butter

a little milk
a little extra butter for topping

To make the lentil base, put the lentils into a large saucepan with
the water and boil gently until tender, about 45 minutes. Drain.
Meanwhile melt the butter in a large saucepan and fry the onion
until tender. Add the garlic, mixed herbs, tomatoes, drained lentils
and parsley. Season with salt and pepper. Spoon the mixture into a
greased shallow ovenproof dish.

While the lentils are cooking, prepare the mashed potato
topping. Put the potatoes into a saucepan, cover with water, and
boil until just tender when pierced with a knife. Drain. Add half the
butter and some salt and pepper, then mash the potatoes until
smooth, adding a little milk to make a smooth, light consistency.

Set the oven to 200°C/400°F/Gas Mark 6. Spoon the potato over
the top of the lentil mixture, then spread it out evenly. Run the
prongs of a fork over the top to make ridges, then dot with a little
butter and bake for 45 minutes, until heated through and golden
brown.

Lentil Salad

If you cook some extra green lentils, they can be made into a good salad. Moisten them with a little vinaigrette dressing, then add a finely chopped onion, some coarsely-grated carrot (which gives a pretty colour) and a tablespoonful or so of chopped parsley or other fresh herbs. Other ingredients such as sliced raw mushrooms, chopped green or red pepper, sliced celery, skinned and chopped tomato or cooked sweetcorn kernels can also be added. Serve with hot wholewheat rolls or pitta bread.

14 Beautiful Beans

Beans are a very useful basic for the thrifty cook. They're healthy, nutritious and can be delicious if they're prepared in an imaginative way. There are many varieties available and it's interesting trying different ones. I've described over thirty of these in my *Bean Book* and my little book of *Beans and Lentils*. For the purposes of this book, I've chosen several tried and trusted ones which are easy to buy, quick and easy to prepare tastily. These are chick peas, red kidney beans, butter beans, bean mix, which is a colourful mixture that you can get at health shops, and, for that traditional favourite, pease pudding, and also a delicious chewy salad, split peas.

The chick peas, red kidney beans and butter beans can be bought dried or in cans. It's cheaper to buy the dried ones and soak and cook them yourself, and worth it if you're cooking for a number of people and/or have a freezer, so that you can save what you don't need. The canned beans are also a good buy, and can form the basis of some very economical meals.

To Prepare Dried Beans

Put the beans into a big saucepan and cover them with their height again in cold water. Leave to soak for 8 hours. Or bring them to the boil, simmer for 2 minutes, then remove from the heat, cover and leave to stand for 1 hour. Drain and rinse the beans, cover them with fresh water, as before, and bring to the boil. Boil them vigorously for 10 minutes, then turn the heat down so that they simmer steadily until tender. That is, 1–1¼ hours, although chick peas can be obstinate and sometimes take 2 hours or so to soften. This usually means they are rather old and dried up. They do not keep for ever, so buy from a shop with a rapid turnover, and use them up within a few months. Black eyed beans do not need soaking (though they can be soaked), and they will cook in 35–40 minutes.

To Microwave Beans

To do the hot quick soak, put the beans into a bowl with water to cover generously. Cover with a plate. Microwave on full power until the water comes to the boil, then continue to microwave for 1 minute. Allow the beans to stand, covered, for 1 hour.

To cook soaked beans, put them into a bowl with enough water to cover them, cover with a plate then microwave on full until tender: 45 minutes for 225 g (8 oz) red kidney beans and bean mix, followed by 15 minutes standing time, covered; 25 minutes on full for 225 g (8 oz) chick peas, plus 10 minutes standing time; 10 minutes for 225 g (8 oz) split peas, plus 10 minutes standing time.

Indigestion

If you find that pulses give you wind, you might like to try this tip which was sent to me by a Canadian reader. She said that she'd suffered for years, but had found that if she boiled beans and lentils without a lid on the pan, so that all the vapours could get out of the pan, they were perfectly all right and she could eat them every day without any problems!

CHICK PEAS

Delicious little beans – or peas – with a very savoury flavour.

Hummus

This is a delectable, creamy dip. Served with warm wholewheat pitta bread or some raw salad items, such as sprigs of raw cauliflower, celery, carrot and spring onion, for dipping in the mixture, this makes a filling main meal for two.

Serves 2 as a main meal, 4 as a starter   300–600 calories in each serving

225 g (8 oz) dried chick peas, soaked and cooked, or 425 g (14 oz) can, drained
½ teaspoon garlic salt or ½ crushed garlic clove
1 tablespoon sesame cream (tahini)

3 tablespoons oil
2 tablespoons lemon juice
salt and freshly ground black pepper

Drain the chick peas, reserving the liquid. Put them into a food processor or blender with all the other ingredients and blend until smooth. If you don't have a blender mash the chick peas as smoothly as possible and then beat in the other ingredients to make a smoothish mixture. Now add as much of the reserved cooking liquid as to make a light, soft consistency like softly whipped cream. If you're using home-cooked chick peas you may need about 7 tablespoons; with canned chick peas, which are usually softer, you may only need 1–2 tablespoonfuls.

Serve the hummus in a small bowl; or, if you want to make it look really good, put it on to a flat plate and spread it out so that it covers the plate and is about 1 cm (½ inch) deep. Pour a little olive oil over the top, then sprinkle with paprika pepper and garnish with lemon slices and black olives. Eat the hummus by breaking off pieces of warmed wholewheat pitta bread and using these to scoop up the delicious creamy mixture.

Chick Peas in Tomato, Herb and Garlic Dressing

Serve this with some crisp lettuce and warm wholewheat rolls for a filling light meal.

Serves 2 as a main-meal salad, 4 as a first course   175–350 calories in each serving

125 g (4 oz) chick peas, soaked, cooked and drained, or 1 425 g (15 oz) can, drained

For the dressing

2 tablespoons finely chopped onion
1 tablespoon wine vinegar
1 teaspoon mustard powder
1 teaspoon sugar
2 tablespoons tomato puree
1 tablespoon chopped fresh parsley

1 tablespoon chopped fresh herbs if available
1 garlic clove, crushed
3 tablespoons olive oil
salt and freshly ground black pepper

Put the chick peas into a bowl. In another bowl, or in a screwtop jar, put all the dressing ingredients and whisk or shake together. Pour the dressing over the chick peas and mix well. Leave for 2–3 hours, if possible, for the chick peas to absorb the flavours.

Middle Eastern Chick Pea Stew

This is easy to make and an excellent dish when aubergines are reasonably priced. Some cooked rice goes well with it. Make a half quantity for two people; for one, it saves time to make a half quantity and serve it once hot, and once cold, with a warm, crusty roll – it makes a pleasant salad.

Serves 4   200 calories in each serving

125 g (4 oz) chick peas, soaked, cooked and drained, or a 425 g (15 oz) can, drained
900 g (2 lb) aubergines
salt

olive or groundnut oil
2 large onions
2 garlic cloves, crushed
425 g (15 oz) can tomatoes
freshly ground black pepper

Cut the aubergines into 1 cm (½ inch) dice, sprinkle with salt, place in a colander, put a weight on top and leave for 30 minutes. Then rinse the aubergines under cold water and squeeze as much liquid out of them as you can. Set the oven to 200°C/400°F/Gas Mark 6. Heat a little oil in a large saucepan and fry the onion for 10 minutes. Then remove the onion from the pan with a draining spoon, and fry the aubergine pieces, until they're crisp and lightly browned, adding more oil if necessary. Put the aubergine and onion into an ovenproof dish, together with the garlic, tomatoes, chick peas and some seasoning. Cover and bake for 40–60 minutes.

Felafel in Pitta Pockets

If you're using canned chick peas, which are softer than home-cooked ones usually, you may need to add a few fresh breadcrumbs to the mixture to make it firm enough to shape. The chopped parsley is important for the flavour. For two people, make a half quantity, using enough beaten egg to bind and the rest for coating. For one person, you could make a quarter quantity, again using enough egg to bind, though if you have a freezer it would be worth making up a half quantity, or even the full amount, and freezing what you don't need.

Serves 4   650 calories in each serving, including pitta bread

225 g (8 oz) chick peas, soaked,
    cooked and drained, or 2
    425 g (15 oz) cans, drained
1 egg
1 large onion, finely chopped
2 tablespoons chopped parsley
1 garlic clove, crushed
1 teaspoon ground coriander

1 teaspoon ground cumin
pinch of chilli powder
salt and freshly ground black
    pepper
flour, beaten egg and dried
    crumbs to coat oil for deep or
    shallow frying

To serve

4 wholemeal pitta breads
2 tomatoes, sliced

½ cucumber, sliced
lemon wedges

Mash the chick peas thoroughly, then add the egg, onion, parsley, garlic and spices. Mix well; season with salt and pepper. Shape into flat circles about 1 cm (½ inch) thick, coat in flour then in egg and breadcrumbs. Put the pitta bread to warm under the grill or in a moderate oven. Put enough oil into a frying pan to cover the base thinly, and when it is hot put in the felafel and fry for 3 minutes on each side, until golden brown. Or deepfry. Drain well on crumpled kitchen paper. Cut each pitta bread in half across the centre, then fill each with felafel, sliced tomato and cucumber and lemon wedges. Or serve the felafel with a salad and a sauce made by stirring some chopped fresh herbs or spring onions into plain yogurt.

RED KIDNEY BEANS

Everyone's favourite, these pretty red beans go well in any vegetable stew and make a delicious salad.

Easy Vegetable and Red Kidney Bean Stew

Serves 4   180 calories in each serving

1 large onion, sliced
1 large red pepper, de-seeded
  and chopped
2 carrots, scraped and diced
2 leeks or medium-sized
  courgettes, sliced
2 sticks of celery, sliced
1 tablespoon vegetable oil
175 g (6 oz) mushrooms,
  washed and sliced

4 tomatoes, skinned and
  quartered
125 g (4 oz) red kidney beans,
  soaked, cooked and drained,
  or a 425 g (15 oz) can, rinsed
  and drained
salt and freshly ground black
  pepper
½ teaspoon paprika

Heat the oil in a large saucepan and add the onion, pepper, carrots, leeks or courgettes and celery. Cook gently for 10 minutes, with a lid on the pan, then add the mushrooms, tomatoes, kidney beans, paprika and some salt and pepper to taste. Cook, covered, for a further 10–15 minutes. Check seasoning and serve. Baked or mashed potatoes go well with this, or crusty wholemeal rolls.

Red Kidney Bean and Tomato Pie

This is a potato-topped pie: simple, quick and easy. A cooked green vegetable such as sprouts or broccoli goes well with it. For two people, simply halve the ingredients and bake the finished pie for 30 minutes; for one person, use a quarter of the quantities — half a 225 g (8 oz) can of tomatoes and half a 225 g (8 oz) can of red kidney beans, and bake for 20 minutes.

Serves 4   440 calories in each serving

2 large onions, peeled and sliced
1 tablespoon vegetable oil
175 g (6 oz) mushrooms,
   washed and sliced (optional)
425 g (15 oz) can tomatoes
125 g (4 oz) red kidney beans,
   soaked, cooked and drained,
   or a 425 g (15 oz) can, rinsed
   and drained

salt and freshly ground black
   pepper
750 g (1½ lb) creamy mashed
   potatoes
4 tablespoons grated cheese

Set the oven to 200°C/400°F/Gas Mark 6. Fry the onion in the oil for 7 minutes, then add the mushrooms, if you're using these, and fry for a further 3 minutes. Remove from the heat and add the tomatoes, beans and seasoning. Spoon the mixture into a shallow ovenproof dish. Spoon the potato on top and spead it evenly covering all the bean mixture. Sprinkle with the grated cheese. Bake for 30–40 minutes, until golden brown on top.

Red Kidney Bean Salad

Serves 2 as a main-meal salad   200 calories in each serving

125 g (4 oz) red kidney beans,
   soaked, cooked and drained,

or a 425 g (15 oz) can,
   drained

For the dressing

2 tablespoons finely chopped
  onion
1 tablespoon wine vinegar
1 teaspoon made mustard
1 teaspoon sugar
2 tablespoons tomato puree
1 tablespoon chopped fresh
  parsley

1 garlic clove, crushed
3 tablespoons olive oil
salt and freshly ground black
  pepper
1 tablespoon chopped parsley

Put the red kidney beans into a bowl. In another bowl, or in a screwtop jar, put all the dressing ingredients except the chopped parsley and whisk or shake together. Pour the dressing over the beans and mix well. Leave for 2–3 hours, if possible, for the beans to absorb the flavours.

BUTTER BEANS

These big, succulent beans absorb other flavours well. Try them in this pretty mixture, which is equally nice hot or cold.

Multicolour Butter Beans

For two people, halve all the quantities; for one person, use a quarter of the quantities, using a 225 g (8 oz) can of butter beans, or 50 g (2 oz) dried ones and 1 celery stick.

Serves 4   230 calories in each serving

3 sticks of celery, cut into 6
   mm (¼ inch) dice
1 small red pepper, de-seeded
   and cut into 6 mm dice
1 tablespoon oil
2 teaspoons curry powder
225 g (8 oz) frozen sweetcorn
   kernels

225 g (8 oz) butter beans,
   soaked, cooked and drained,
   or 2 425 g (15 oz) cans,
   drained
salt and freshly ground black
   pepper
chopped parsley

Fry the celery and red pepper in the oil in a large saucepan for 10 minutes, until soft but not browned. Add the curry powder and stir for 1 minute, then add the sweetcorn and butter beans and cook over a gentle heat for a further 4–5 minutes, until everything is heated through. Season with salt and pepper, sprinkle with chopped parsley. Potatoes baked in their jackets go well with this, and it's nice cold as well as hot.

Butter Beans, Green Peppers and Tomatoes Au Gratin

This is easy, tasty and colourful. For two people, simply halve the ingredients and bake the finished pie for 30 minutes; for one person, use a quarter of the quantities – half a 225 g (8 oz) can of tomatoes and half a 225 g (8 oz) can of red kidney beans, and bake for 20 minutes.

Serves 4   350 calories in each serving

2 large onions, peeled and sliced
1 green pepper, de-seeded and
  sliced
1 tablespoon oil
1 garlic clove, crushed
225 g (8 oz) butter beans,
  soaked, cooked and drained,
  or 2 425 g (15 oz) cans,
  drained

425 g (15 oz) can tomatoes
salt and freshly ground black
  pepper
125 g (4 oz) grated cheese

Fry the onions and pepper in the oil in a large saucepan for 10 minutes, until soft but not browned. Add the garlic, butter beans, tomatoes and seasoning to taste. Prepare a hot grill. Put the butter bean mixture into the grill pan, or a shallow heatproof dish which will fit under the grill. Sprinkle the grated cheese evenly over the top. Grill until the cheese has melted and is golden brown. Serve at once, with crusty bread.

BEAN MIX

The bean mix which I particularly like, because of its pretty colours is Holland & Barrett's 'de luxe' bean mix, but any bean mix would do, or you could make up your own by mixing equal quantities of, say, red kidney beans, black beans, flageolet beans, black eye beans and pinto beans. Make up a quarter or half of this mixture for one or two people.

Technicolour Bean Salad

Serves 4   250 calories in each serving

225 g (8 oz) Holland &
  Barrett's de luxe bean mix, or
  any mixture of beans
1 medium-sized mild onion,
  peeled and finely chopped
1 garlic clove, crushed

½ teaspoon made mustard
1 tablespoon red wine vinegar
3 tablespoons olive oil
salt and freshly ground black
  pepper
4 tablespoons chopped parsley

Soak the beans in plenty of cold water overnight. Next day, drain and rinse them, then put them into a saucepan with their height again in cold water and bring to the boil. Boil the beans hard for 10 minutes, then turn the heat down and let them simmer for 1 hour or so until they are tender. Drain and add the onion. Mix together the garlic, mustard, vinegar, oil and a little salt and pepper; add this to the bean mixture and stir well. Leave the beans to cool, stirring them from time to time, then add the parsley. Serve with crusty rolls, or on a base of lettuce.

SPLIT PEAS

Split peas can be made into the traditional 'pease pudding' or a chewy and unusual salad. They do not need soaking before cooking.

Pease Pudding

This is pleasant with gravy, mint sauce, crispy golden roast potatoes and a cooked green vegetable, as a vegetarian Sunday lunch. These quantities make quite a large amount, but if there's any over, it's good dipped in beaten egg or milk and dried crumbs, fried until crisp and served with mint or apple sauce. Make a quarter quantity (with one egg) or half quantity for one or two people and bake for 20–30 minutes.

Serves 4   470 calories in each serving

450 g (1 lb) yellow split peas
2 large onions, peeled and
    chopped
50 g (2 oz) butter
2 teaspoons fennel seeds
    (optional)

salt and freshly ground black
    pepper
2 eggs (optional)

Put the split peas into a saucepan, cover with water and cook gently until soft – this takes about 30 minutes or so. Drain. Set oven to 180°C/ 350°F/Gas Mark 4. (Or, if you have roast potatoes in the oven, cooking at a higher temperature, the pease pudding can go into the oven on a low shelf – the temperature isn't crucial.) Fry the onions in the butter for 10 minutes and stir in the fennel seeds if you're using them, and the eggs, if you're using these. Season. Spoon the mixture into a lightly-greased fairly shallow ovenproof dish and bake for 50–60 minutes, until browned on top.

Green and Yellow Split Pea Salad with Lemon

This salad is especially nice made with half yellow and half dried split green peas, which you may have to go to the health shop to get. The important thing with this salad is to undercook the peas, so that they don't break up. Serve with some soft wholemeal rolls.

Serves 4   250 calories in each serving

125 g (4 oz) dried split yellow peas
125 g (4 oz) dried split green peas
pared or grated rind of ½ lemon
1 garlic clove, crushed
½ teaspoon made mustard
1 tablespoon red wine vinegar

3 tablespoons olive oil
salt and freshly ground black
    pepper
1 tablespoon chopped mint if
    available

Put both lots of peas into a pan, cover with plenty of water and cook until just tender, about 15–20 minutes. Don't let them get at all mushy. Drain well and add the lemon rind. Mix together the garlic, mustard, vinegar, oil and a little salt and pepper; add this to the split peas, together with the mint, if you have it. Stir well, then leave to cool, stirring from time to time.

15 Great Grains

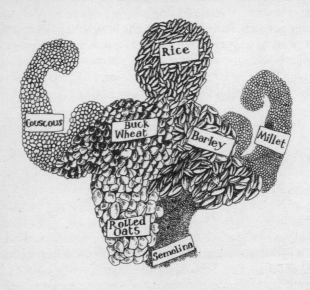

Grains are cheap and nourishing. Although we usually think of them as starchy 'fillers', they actually contain quite a lot of protein, as well as B vitamins and minerals such as iron, so that they can easily become main courses. They're also easy to cook.

There are quite a number of grains and although rice is probably the most useful, it's worth trying some of the more unusual ones such as millet and bulgur wheat, which you can get at the health shop, for variety. Left-over grains are useful because they make a good base for rissoles, stuffings or salads – just add small quantities of tasty ingredients such as fried onion or mushrooms, garlic and herbs, chopped hardboiled egg or nuts, and you've practically got another meal.

RICE

Rice for savoury dishes should be the long-grained variety, and you don't need to pay extra for treated, quick-cook or easy-cook rice. All rice is easy to cook, and you shouldn't find you have any problems. I prefer brown rice because of its nutty flavour and chewy texture, and the extra B vitamins and fibre which it contains.

BASIC COOKING OF BROWN RICE

There are two methods, and each have their devotees, but I think both work equally well, so it's really a question of which one you like best.

The fast-boiling, lots of water, method: For this method you need to half fill a large saucepan with water, bring to the boil and add a teaspoonful of salt. Throw in the rice, allowing 50 g (2 oz) per person if the rice is to accompany something else, or up to 100 g (4 oz) each if the rice is more or less the main dish, without much else. Let the rice boil away, without a lid on the pan, for 20–30 minutes, until the rice is tender. Drain the rice into a colander and rinse it under the hot tap to remove any starch. Then tip it back into the saucepan and dry the rice off over a low heat for about 5 minutes, stirring it several times to prevent sticking. The rice can also be dried off (and kept warm) in a cool oven. Put the rice into a shallow ovenproof dish and place, uncovered, in the oven for about 10 minutes.

The slow-cook, not much water, method: For this you need to measure both the rice and the water, and it's handy to use the same container for this – a large mug, or a 300 ml (½ pint) measure. Choose a medium-sized saucepan which has a close-fitting lid, if possible. You can fry an onion in a tablespoonful of oil before putting in the rice, for extra flavour, if you like, and spices such as cloves, turmeric and cinnamon stick can be added, too, for a spiced rice. Put one measure of rice into a saucepan, on top of the onion, if you're using this, and add two measures of water and a teaspoonful of salt. Bring the water to the boil, then put the lid on the pan (or cover closely with a piece of foil and/or an old plate), and turn the heat right down as low as it will go. Leave the rice, without peeking or stirring, until it's tender and all the water has been absorbed, which takes 45 minutes.

To cook rice in the microwave: Put the rice into a microwave-proof container with water and a little salt, using the proportions of 1 cup of rice to 2 cups of water. Cover with a plate. Microwave on full power, without stirring, for 25 minutes. Leave to stand, still covered, for 10 minutes, then fluff with a fork and use.

Rice Salad

Rice salad is easy to make and can be exactly what you want it to be: just add the ingredients to the cooked rice. The more contrast you can get in the colour, texture and flavour of the ingredients you add, the better. Chopped raw onion or spring onion, small cubes of cucumber, chopped red or green pepper, sweetcorn kernels, cooked peas, small cubes of cooked carrot or coarsely grated raw carrot, finely chopped celery, raisins or sultanas, finely chopped dried apricots, chopped nuts, chopped skinned tomato, cooked beans such as red kidney beans or chick peas, black olives, chopped fresh herbs. A lightly-curried version is nice: you make this by frying an onion in some oil with a little curry powder, and stirring that into the rice, together with some diced apple, sliced banana, roasted peanuts and finely chopped hardboiled eggs. Add your chosen ingredients, moisten the mixture with a little vinaigrette dressing or a spoonful or two of good quality mayonnaise thinned with some milk. Check the seasoning, then spoon the salad into a serving dish and garnish with some chopped parsley, chives or black olives.

Rice and Courgette Gratin

This delicious recipe was given to me by a French friend and is an old family one from Provence. Make half these quantities for one or two people. If there's any over, it's good cold, with salad, or as a filling for green peppers or big tomatoes. See pages 103 and 107 for how to prepare these.

Serves 3–4   420–560 calories in each serving

225 g (8 oz) brown rice
1 large onion, peeled and
   chopped
4 courgettes, diced
2 tablespoons oil

125 g (4 oz) grated cheese
1 egg
salt and freshly ground black
   pepper

Cook the rice by either of the above methods, until tender. Drain, if necessary. Meanwhile set the oven to 180°C/350°F/Gas Mark 4 and fry the onion and courgettes in the oil for 15–20 minutes, until very soft. Add the rice, half the cheese, the egg and salt and pepper to taste. Spoon the mixture into a shallow ovenproof dish, sprinkle with the rest of the cheese, and bake in the oven for about 45 minutes, or longer if you like: this is delicious really well cooked to a deep golden brown. It goes well with a sliced tomato salad or some green salad.

Vegetable Rice with Roasted Nuts

The turmeric colours the rice pale yellow and the vegetables and roasted nuts look pretty against it. A variation is to use a can of drained red kidney beans instead of the nuts – add them with the tomatoes. The amount of liquid added to this doesn't follow the 'double the amount of liquid to the amount of grain' rule because of the vegetables, which make the mixture more liquid, so less water is used. If you're cooking for two people, use half these quantities; for one person, I suggest using half the quantities and serving this once hot with a salad, and once cold, with hot garlic bread.

Serves 4   450 calories in each serving

1 tablespoon olive oil
1 onion, peeled and chopped
1 garlic clove, crushed
225 g (8 oz) brown rice
425 ml (¾ pint) water
½ teaspoon turmeric
1 teaspoon salt
1 large carrot, scraped and
  diced
1 red pepper, de-seeded and
  chopped

225 g (8 oz) green beans or
  leeks, cut into 2 cm (1 inch)
  pieces
4 tomatoes, skinned and sliced
freshly ground black pepper
125 g (4 oz) roasted nuts –
  peanuts or cashew nuts
chopped parsley

Fry the onion in the oil in a large saucepan for 10 minutes, until soft but not browned, then add the turmeric and garlic. Stir for a moment or two, then add the rice, water and salt. Bring up to the boil, then turn the heat right down, put a lid on the pan, and leave to cook for 20 minutes. After 20 minutes, lift off the lid and put the carrots, pepper and green beans or leeks in on top of the rice: don't stir them in. Cover again, and cook for a further 20 minutes. Then add the tomatoes, some freshly grated pepper and roasted nuts. Stir gently to mix everything, then serve at once, sprinkled with chopped parsley. This is nice with a simple salad, such as watercress.

If there's any over, it's lovely cold, like a rice salad – or can be used to stuff peppers.

Left-Over Rice Dish

This is simple but good; it's almost worth making sure there's some rice left over, in order to make it! Use half these quantities for two people, quarter quantities for one, which means using 3 level teaspoons of flour for the sauce.

Serves 4   550 calories in each serving

350 g–450 g (12 oz–1 lb) (about
    2 cupfuls) left-over cooked
    rice
6 hardboiled eggs, sliced
50 g (2 oz) butter
1–2 teaspoons curry powder

2 rounded tablespoons flour
600 g (1 pint) milk
salt and freshly ground black
    pepper
a drop or two of tabasco sauce

Put the rice and eggs into a shallow heatproof casserole dish and warm them through in a cool oven (170°C/325°F/Gas Mark 3). Make a sauce: melt the butter in a medium-sized saucepan and stir in the curry powder and flour; cook for a moment or two, then add the milk and stir over the heat until smooth. Let the sauce simmer over a gentle heat for 10–15 minutes, to cook the flour. Then season with salt and pepper and add a dash of tabasco sauce. Pour the sauce over the rice and eggs and serve piping hot. (And if there's any of that over, it makes excellent croquettes!)

Spiced Rice

Some spiced rice makes a pleasant, money-saving meal served either just with a tomato salad or with a curry sauce. The ingredients can be halved; the cooking time remains the same.

Serves 4 with a curry, 2 as a main course with salad
240 calories in each serving

1 tablespoon oil or soft butter
225 g (8 oz) brown rice (or a
*   300 ml (½ pint) measure full)*
1 teaspoon turmeric
3 cloves
2–3 cardamom pods if available

2 cm (1 inch) piece of cinnamon
*   stick, if available*
salt and freshly ground black
*   pepper*
600 ml (1 pint) boiling water

Heat the oil or butter in a medium-sized saucepan then add the rice. Fry the rice over a gentle heat for 5 minutes, stirring. Then add the spices and some salt and pepper and stir for 1–2 minutes. Finally add the water – stand back, it will sizzle – bring up to the boil, then cover the pan, turn the heat down and leave to cook very gently for 45 minutes, after which all the water should have been absorbed. If it hasn't, just leave the rice to stand, covered but off the heat, for a further 10–15 minutes. Fluff the rice by stirring gently with a fork, and serve.

Basic Curry Sauce for Serving with Rice

This curry sauce makes a base for any vegetables which you may have, or it can be used on its own, over plain boiled rice or the spiced rice above. Halve the amount for one or two people.

Serves 4   80 calories in each serving

25 g (1 oz) butter
1 large onion, peeled and
*   chopped*
walnut-sized piece fresh ginger,
*   grated*
2 garlic cloves, crushed
1 bay leaf

1 tablespoon ground coriander
1 tablespoon ground cumin
pinch of chilli powder
225 g (8 oz) can tomatoes
1 teaspoon salt
freshly ground black pepper
60 ml (1 pint) water

Heat the butter in a large saucepan and fry the onion for 7–8 minutes, then add the garlic, bay leaf and spices and stir over the heat for 2–3 minutes. Add the tomatoes, salt, some pepper and the water. Let the sauce simmer gently for about 30 minutes.

If you're adding raw vegetables, such as cubes of potato, or slices of carrot, put them in with the tomatoes; quicker-cooking vegetables, such as cauliflower, peas, or a little shredded white cabbage, and also left-over cooked vegetables, are best added about 10 minutes before the end of cooking time.

Egg Curry

For egg curry, add 4–6 quartered hard-boiled eggs to the curry sauce about 10 minutes before you serve the curry and sprinkle with some desiccated coconut.

Rice Croquettes

These are delicious, crisp on the outside and tender inside. Serve them with some sliced tomatoes and mango chutney; or a sauce made by stirring some chopped herbs or spring onion into some plain yogurt. Use half these quantities to make enough for one or two people, with half a beaten egg to bind and half to coat the outside of the croquettes.

Serves 3–4   380–490 calories in each serving

350 g (12 oz) (or about 2 cupfuls) cooked rice
2 hard-boiled eggs, finely chopped
2 tablespoons chopped fresh parsley
4 tablespoons grated cheese
1 egg
curry powder
salt and freshly ground black pepper

To coat

1 egg, beaten with 1 tablespoon	*dried crumbs*
cold water	*oil for shallow frying*

Mix together the rice, hard-boiled egg, parsley, grated cheese and raw egg. Add enough curry powder to give the mixture a spicy lift – ½–1 teaspoonful, perhaps – and salt and pepper to taste. Form the mixture into croquettes about the size of golf balls, dip them into beaten egg, then into dried crumbs. Pour enough oil into a frying pan to cover the base lightly, and set over a moderate heat. When the oil is hot, put in the croquettes and fry them, turning them around with a palette knife so that they get browned all over. Drain them on kitchen paper. Serve at once.

OATS

Rolled oats – the ordinary 'porridge' oats which you can buy at any supermarket – can be used to make a quick and easy savoury. You can also make your own homemade muesli mix from these much more cheaply (and I think better) than buying a made-up one. Just put 2 cupfuls of porridge oats into a bowl and add ½ cupful of raisins and ½ cupful of nuts and mix together. The nicest nuts to use, I think, are hazelnuts. Buy the kind which still have their skins on (from health shops), and roast them as described on page 126, then chop them coarsely.

Quick Oat Savoury

This couldn't be quicker or easier. For one person, simply halve the quantities and bake for about 20 minutes. For four people, double the ingredients and bake for about 40 minutes.

Serves 2   420 calories in each serving

4 heaped tablespoons rolled oats	*450 g (1 lb) tomatoes, skinned and chopped, plus 3–4*
100 g (4 oz) grated cheese	*tablespoons milk, or a 425 g (15 oz) can*

Set the oven to 200°C/400°F/Gas Mark 6. Grease a shallow ovenproof dish. Put half the oats into the base of the dish, followed by half the tomatoes, then half the grated cheese. Repeat the layers. Sprinkle with the milk if you're using fresh tomatoes. Bake for 30 minutes, until the oats have absorbed the moisture and the dish is golden brown on top. A crunchy salad, such as cabbage and carrot, goes well with this.

BARLEY

Barley is cheap and has a pleasant flavour which makes a change from rice. The kind of barley I prefer is the pearl barley which you can get at any supermarket. Although this has been refined to some extent, it still contains a lot of fibre, and is actually a better source of this than brown rice! You can cook it in the same way as rice and serve it as an accompaniment or the basis of a main dish or salad, with other vegetables and flavourings added. I think it's nicest in its more traditional role, as a filling ingredient in soups and stews.

Barley Casserole

Quarter or halve the quantities to make enough for one or two people.

Serves 4   360 calories in each serving

2 tablespoons oil
1 large onion, peeled and
  chopped
4 large carrots, scraped and
  sliced
450 g (1 lb) leeks, washed and
  cut into 2 cm (1 inch) pieces
2 large potatoes, peeled and cut
  into 2 cm (1 inch) chunks
2 garlic cloves, crushed
100 g (4 oz) (or ½ cup) pearl
  barley

1 litre (1¾ pints) water
1 tablespoon stock powder
2 tablespoons soy sauce
100–225 g (4–8 oz)
  mushrooms, sliced (optional)
salt and freshly ground black
  pepper
chopped parsley, to serve, if
  available

Heat the oil in a large saucepan. Add the onion and fry for 5 minutes, then put in the carrots, leeks, potatoes and garlic and fry for a further 5 minutes. Add the barley, stir well, then add the water and stock powder. Bring to the boil, then simmer for about 30 minutes, until the vegetables and barley are tender. Add the soy sauce and mushrooms and cook for a further 4–5 minutes, then check seasoning and serve, sprinkled with some chopped parsley, if you have any.

MILLET

Millet, usually thought of as budgie-food, actually makes quite good people-food and is a pleasant change from rice. You can buy it at a health shop and it's a useful grain if you're at all anaemic, as it's a good source of iron. You can cook it exactly like rice, using the slow-cook method, and the millet will only take 20 minutes. It tastes best if you roast it a bit before adding the water – just put the millet into a dry saucepan and stir it over the heat for 3 minutes or so until the millet starts to smell beautifully 'roasted' and some of the grains start to 'pop' and jump around.

Spicy Millet Pilaf

Serve this with a crunchy salad. If there's any over, add an egg, make the mixture into flat burgers, coat in beaten egg and crumbs, and shallow-fry. To make this for one person, use a quarter of the quantities; for two people use half. Cook for the same length of time.

Serves 4   500 calories in each serving, including almonds

350 g (12 oz) (or 1½ cups) millet
2 tablespoons oil
1 large onion, peeled and
*   chopped*
2 carrots, diced
1 garlic clove, crushed
walnut-sized piece of fresh
*   ginger, grated*

2 cm (1 inch) cinnamon stick, if
*   available*
700 ml (1¼ pint) (or 3 cups)
*   water*
salt and freshly ground black
*   pepper*
50 g (2 oz) raisins and 50 g (2 oz)
*   flaked almonds (optional)*

First roast the millet by putting it into a large saucepan and stirring over a moderate heat for 3–4 minutes, until it begins to smell roasted and some of the grains start to 'pop'. Remove from the heat and tip the millet into a bowl for the moment. Now heat the oil in the saucepan and fry the onion and carrots for about 7 minutes. Add the garlic, ginger and cinnamon and stir for a moment or two, then add the millet and stir so that everything is mixed together. Add the water and some salt and pepper. Bring up to the boil, then cover the saucepan, turn down the heat and leave the millet to cook very gently for 15–20 minutes, until all the water has been absorbed. Fluff the millet with a fork and add the nuts and raisins if you're using these.

BULGUR WHEAT

This is sometimes called Burghul wheat and is a precooked grain, so it doesn't need much cooking. In fact it can just be soaked, 1 cup of wheat to 2 cups of hot or cold water, left for 10–15 minutes, until the water has been absorbed, and used. You can make a very good Middle Eastern salad, Tabbouleh, by adding skinned and chopped tomatoes, some chopped raw onion and lots of chopped parsley and mint, and some lemon juice, olive oil, salt and pepper to soaked bulgur wheat. For most savoury dishes, however, the wheat needs to be heated after soaking; you can do this by putting it into a greased ovenproof dish and heating in a moderate oven, or you can do the soaking and cooking processes in one go by cooking the wheat by the slow-cook rice method. Cooked bulgur wheat makes a good accompaniment to other dishes as a change from rice. Or it can be made into a delicious pilaf with a Middle Eastern flavour.

Bulgur Pilaf

As with the vegetable rice, less liquid than usual is used (1½ times the amount of grain instead of 2 times) because of the moisture which the vegetables contribute. Use half these quantities for one or two servings.

Serves 3–4   400–550 calories in each serving

1 large onion, peeled and
   chopped
1 red pepper, de-seeded and
   chopped
2 tablespoons oil
1 garlic clove, crushed
2 cm (1 inch) cinnamon stick, if
   available
walnut-sized piece of fresh
   ginger, grated

225 g (8 oz) (or 1 cup) bulgur
   wheat
300 ml (¾) pint (or 1¼ cups)
   water
salt and freshly ground black
   pepper
50 g (2 oz) raisins
50 g (2 oz) flaked almonds or
   roasted peanuts for economy

166

Fry the onion and red pepper in the oil in a medium-sized saucepan for about 7 minutes. Then add the garlic, ginger and cinnamon and stir for a moment or two. Add the bulgur wheat and stir, then pour in the water and some salt and pepper. Bring up to the boil, then cover the saucepan, turn down the heat and leave to cook very gently for 10–15 minutes, until all the water has been absorbed. Fluff with a fork and add the nuts and raisins.

Bulgur Pilaf with Red Lentils

Bulgur wheat and red lentils cook in about the same amount of time and together make a tasty and filling combination. A sliced tomato salad goes well with this. Halve the ingredients for two people; quarter them for one, using the same cooking times.

Serves 4   360 calories in each serving

1 large onion, peeled and chopped	600 ml (1 pint) (or 2 cups) water
2 tablespoons oil	salt and freshly ground black pepper
2 garlic cloves, crushed	
walnut-sized piece of fresh ginger, grated	2 heaped tablespoons chopped parsley
225 g (8 oz) (or 1 cup) bulgur wheat	1 tablespoon lemon juice
125 g (4 oz) (or ½ cup) split red lentils	

Fry the onion in the oil in a medium-sized saucepan for about 7 minutes. Then add the garlic and ginger and stir for a moment or two. Add the bulgur wheat and lentils and stir, then pour in the water and some salt and pepper. Bring up to the boil, then cover the saucepan, turn down the heat and leave to cook very gently for 30 minutes, until all the water has been absorbed and the lentils are pale and tender. With a fork gently stir in the parsley and add lemon juice, salt and pepper to taste.

BUCKWHEAT

Buckwheat has a strong flavour, not to everyone's taste, but it's an economical, healthy grain, and certainly worth a try. Buy roasted buckwheat, which you can get at any health shop, and cook it by the slow-cook rice method. Flavour it with plenty of fried onion, crushed garlic and soy sauce. Mushrooms and carrots also go well with buckwheat, as in this recipe:

Buckwheat Bake

Serve this with a cooked green vegetable such as sprouts or spinach. Use half these quantities for two people, a quarter to make enough for one.

Serves 4   320 calories in each serving

2 tablespoons oil
2 large onions, peeled and
   chopped
450 g (1 lb) carrots, sliced into
   rings
1 garlic clove, crushed
125 g (4 oz) mushrooms,
   washed and chopped

225 g (8oz) (or 1 cupful) roasted
   buckwheat
2 teaspoons mixed herbs
300 ml (¾ pint) water
salt and freshly ground black
   pepper
2 tablespoons soy sauce
2 tablespoons chopped parsley

Heat the oil in the saucepan and fry the onion and carrots for about 7 minutes. Add the garlic and mushrooms and fry for 2–3 minutes, then add the buckwheat, herbs, water and some salt and pepper. Bring to the boil, then cover and leave to cook gently for 30 minutes, until all the water has been absorbed and the carrots are tender. Add the soy sauce and parsley, check the seasoning, and serve.

COUSCOUS

Another pre-cooked grain, actually a type of semolina, couscous is one of my favourites, and very easy to use. Like bulgur wheat, it only needs to be soaked in water, 1 cup couscous to 2 cups of water, for about 10 minutes, until all the water has been absorbed, then heated through. The easiest way to do this is to put the couscous into a steamer, metal colander or sieve set over a saucepan of steaming stew. The couscous is then served with the stew. Alternatively, the couscous can be heated over a saucepan of steaming water for about 10 minutes, or put into a greased casserole, covered, and heated through in a coolish oven. In the Middle East, couscous is usually served with a spicy chick pea stew, as in the following recipe.

Couscous with Spicy Chick Pea Stew

As a change from chick peas, frozen sweetcorn kernels, broad beans or cut green beans can be used instead. Use a quarter of these ingredients to make couscous for one person, or half if you're cooking for two.

Serves 4   530–800 calories in each serving

450 g (1 lb) couscous
½ teaspoon salt dissolved in
   600 ml (1 pint) warm water

2 tablespoons olive oil

For the spiced vegetable stew

2 tablespoons olive oil
2 onions, peeled and chopped
225 g (8 oz) carrots, scraped
  and diced
225 g (8 oz) courgettes, diced
2 teaspoons each cinnamon,
  ground cumin and ground
  coriander
4 tablespoons tomato puree
125 g (4 oz) raisins or sweetcorn
  kernels

225 g (8 oz) dried chick peas,
  soaked, cooked until tender
  then drained, or 2 × 425 g
  (15 oz) cans, drained
900 ml (1½ pints) water
salt and freshly ground black
  pepper
2 tablespoons chopped parsley

Soak the couscous in water as described above. Leave on one side. Heat the oil in a large saucepan or saucepan part of a steamer, add the onion and carrot and fry gently for 10 minutes, then stir in the spices and tomato puree and cook for 2–3 minutes, stirring. Put in the courgettes, raisins or sweetcorn and the chick peas and water. Bring to the boil, then turn the heat down so that the stew just simmers. By this time the couscous will have absorbed all the water. Put it into the steamer, metal colander or sieve, breaking it up a bit with your fingers again as you do so. (If the chosen container has large holes, it may be necessary to line it with a piece of cloth, to prevent the grains falling through, but I have never found this necessary.) Put the steamer, colander or sieve over the stew, cover with a lid or plate, and leave for 25–30 minutes. Season to taste. Stir the olive oil into the couscous, then put the couscous onto a large, warmed serving dish, pour the stew into the centre, sprinkle with chopped parsley and serve at once.

SEMOLINA

Semolina makes the basis of two delicious savoury dishes, definite 'stars' in the thrifty cook's repertoire. Incidentally, if you want to make both of these semolina dishes from one batch of mixture, use the basic mixture given for cheese fritters, spread it out as described and leave until cold. Then use half the mixture for cheese fritters, and cut the rest into circles and complete as described for Italian Gnocchi.

Italian Gnocchi

This is a little bit more trouble than some of the dishes in this book, but it can be made in stages and is cheap and delicious. For one person use a quarter of these quantities and 1 egg; for two people, use half, also with 1 egg. Bake for the time given.

Serves 4   340 calories in each serving

600 ml (1 pint) milk
4 heaped tablespoons semolina
1 small egg
75 g (3 oz) grated Parmesan
*   cheese*

15 g (½ oz) butter
salt, freshly ground black
*   pepper and nutmeg*

Put the milk into a large saucepan and bring to the boil. Then sprinkle the semolina gradually over the top of the milk, beating well after each addition – a wire balloon whisk is good for this. When all the semolina has been added, let the mixture simmer gently for 5 minutes. Then remove from the heat and beat in the egg and two thirds of the cheese. Season with salt, pepper and nutmeg. Spread the mixture into a lightly-oiled shallow tin or onto a plate, so that it is about 8 mm (⅓ inch) deep. Leave to get completely cold, then cut the mixture into squares, or into circles using a pastry cutter. First put the trimmings into a shallow dish, then arrange the circles on top. Dot with the butter, sprinkle with the remaining cheese and put under a hot grill until the top is golden brown and the inside heated through. This is good served with a watercress or tomato salad.

Cheese Fritters

Another savoury dish made from semolina, these are a bit fiddly to make, though you can do them in stages. They are cheap and delicious. I usually serve them with homemade parsley sauce, made as described on page 28. Even if you're cooking for one or two people, I recommend making the full quantity if you've got a freezer. If not, these quantities will halve or quarter satisfactorily.

Serves 4   560 calories in each serving

600 ml (1 pint) milk
1 small onion, peeled and stuck
   with 3–4 cloves of garlic
1 bay leaf
4 heaped tablespoons semolina

125 g (4 oz) grated cheese
½ teaspoon dry mustard
salt and freshly ground black
   pepper

To coat

1 large egg, beaten with 1
   tablespoon water

dried crumbs
oil for shallow frying

To serve

slices of lemon, sprigs of parsley

Put the milk, onion and bay leaf into a saucepan and bring the milk to the boil. Then remove from the heat, cover and leave for 10–15 minutes, for the flavours to infuse. Remove the onion and bayleaf. Bring the milk back to the boil, then sprinkle the semolina over the top, stirring all the time. Let the mixture simmer for about 5 minutes, to cook the semolina, then remove from the heat and beat in the cheese, mustard and seasoning to taste. Spread the mixture out on an oiled plate or baking tray so that it's about 1 cm (½ inch) deep. Smooth the top, then leave until completely cold. Cut into pieces; dip each first in beaten egg and then in dried crumbs. Shallow fry in hot oil until crisp on both sides, drain well on kitchen towels. Serve at once, garnished with lemon slices and parsley sprigs.

16 Pleasing Puddings

When you're trying to save money, puddings somehow become more important. For one thing, they turn a cheap and rather 'thin' dish into a complete meal. Potato soup, for instance, followed by rhubarb crumble; or baked potatoes followed by apple charlotte, or nutty cabbage salad with baked egg custard afterwards. Fresh fruit, of course, always makes a quick, easy and healthy pudding and can work out very cheaply if you buy fruit in season.

FRESH FRUIT BASE

Fruit Salad

This can be made with whatever fruit is in season and the best value; aim for a pretty mixture of colours. If you're making this for two people, halve the ingredients; for one person, quarter the ingredients, leaving out either the apple or the orange.

Serves 4   80–100 calories in each serving

2 oranges
225 g (8 oz) strawberries, hulled
    and washed or black grapes,
    halved and de-seeded, or
    blackberries or raspberries
2 kiwi fruit, peeled and sliced
    into rounds or 1–2 bananas,
    peeled and sliced

2 apples, cored and sliced,
    unpeeled if skin is good
150 ml (5 fl oz) orange or apple
    juice

Holding the oranges over a bowl and using a sharp knife, cut away
the peel and white pith, using a sawing action and cutting round
and round as if peeling an apple to produce a long piece of peel.
Then cut the orange sections away from the white inner skin. Put
the orange sections into the bowl and add the rest of the fruit and
the orange or apple juice. Serve plain, or with thick yogurt.

Orange Compote

This makes a refreshing and economical pudding when oranges are
cheap.

Serves 4   60–80 calories in each serving

6–8 large oranges

Scrub one of the oranges thoroughly then remove some thin strips
of peel. Use a zester if you have one, otherwise shave off thin strips
of peel with a knife or potato peeler and shred them up. Cut the
peel and pith off the oranges by peeling them thickly with a knife,
holding the oranges over a bowl as you do so to catch any juice.
Then cut the segments away from the inner membranes and put the
segments into the bowl. A variation is to crunch up some of those
sesame snaps which you can get at health shops and some supermarkets and sprinkle them over the top; or make some golden

caramel and scatter this on top. To make caramel, put 2 rounded tablespoons sugar into a heavy-based saucepan over a very low heat until it turns liquid and golden brown. Tilt the pan from side to side so that all the sugar melts, but be very careful not to let it get dark brown or it will taste burnt and bitter. Immediately remove from the heat and pour the caramel on to a sheet of greased greaseproof or non-stick paper. Leave to cool, then break up into shreds and sprinkle on top of the oranges. Serve at once. (To clean the pan, just fill it with water when it has cooled, and heat: the sticky caramel will dissolve and come off the sides of the pan.)

Bananas with Ginger

Very simple, this is just a sliced banana per person, topped with chopped crystallized ginger. Some single cream goes well with it.

Honeyed Pears

This made by peeling, coring.and thinly slicing 1 or 1½ ripe pears per person, then pouring over 1–2 teaspoons clear honey dissolved in 2–3 tablespoons boiling water. A pinch of cinamon or ginger can be added.

BASIC STEWED AND BAKED FRUITS

Many fruits, such as apples, rhubarb, currants, gooseberries, plums and blackberries, if you have the time to pick them, work out cheaply when in season, but need to be cooked before eating. Dried fruits, such as apricots and the dried fruit salad mixture which you can buy at health shops and supermarkets, are quite expensive, but go a long way so can be good value as well as being very nourishing.

Here are the guidelines for baking and stewing these fruits, and some suggestions for turning them into interesting puddings.

Baked Apples

Beautifully easy and cheap when apples are in season. Try filling the cavities with different ingredients; a mixture of ripe blackberries and brown sugar is delicious, so is clear honey mixed with ground almonds, or whole cooking dates, or raisins or sultanas.

60–80 calories in each serving, excluding filling

1 large cooking apple per person

filling ingredients as suggested above

Wash the apples and remove the core leaving the apple whole. Using a sharp knife, score round the apple, just cutting the skin, so that when the apple expands during cooking, the skin won't burst. Set oven to 180°C/350°F/Gas Mark 4. Put the apples into a lightly-greased ovenproof dish or baking tin and fill the cavities with your chosen ingredients, packing them in well. Bake for 45–60 minutes, until the apples are soft and puffed up. Serve hot, with milk, natural yogurt or single cream.

Stewed Apples

Use a quarter of these quantities for one person, half for two.

Serves 4   100 calories in each serving, excluding sugar

900 g (2 lb) cooking apples, peeled, cored and sliced

15 g (½ oz) butter sugar or honey

Put the apples into a saucepan with the butter. Cook over a gentle heat for 7–10 minutes, until the apples are tender. Remove from the heat, sweeten to taste. For an apple puree, beat with a wooden spoon, or, for a smooth, luxurious result, push the mixture through a nylon sieve.

A pleasant variation is to add a handful of raisins or sultanas and ½ teaspoon of mixed spice or ground cloves to the apples at the beginning of the cooking time; the grated rind of a well-scrubbed orange or lemon is also nice in this: add it when you sweeten the mixture. In the late summer, try adding some blackberries to the apple mixture: add them at the beginning of the cooking time.

Stewed Rhubarb, Gooseberries, Blackberries or Blackcurrants

Serves 4   140 calories in each serving

900 g (2 lb) rhubarb, washed and cut into chunks, or gooseberries, 'topped and tailed' or blackcurrants – remove the stems if you are planning to eat the blackcurrants whole, leave them on if you're going to sieve them.

2 rounded tablespoons sugar

Put the fruit into a saucepan and add the sugar. Cook over a very gentle heat for about 15 minutes, until the fruit is tender but not broken up. Check the mixture and add some more sugar if necessary.

Stewed Plums

Stew these in the same way as rhubarb, gooseberries and blackcurrants, adding 2 tablespoons of water to the pan with the fruit. Large plums

178

can be halved and the stones removed first; damsons are better left whole for people to remove the stones themselves when they eat the fruit.

Stewed Dried Fruit

Allow 125 g (4 oz) for each person. A very easy way of treating dried apricots is not to stew them at all but to wash them, cover them with cold water and leave them in the fridge for use as required – they make a good nibble. Otherwise, wash the fruit, cover with boiling water and leave to soak overnight. Next day put the fruit and water into a saucepan, bring to the boil and let it simmer gently for 20–30 minutes, until it feels tender when pierced with a knife, and the liquid has reduced and become syrupy. Remove from the heat and use hot or cold. For a special occasion, add a little brandy while the fruits are still hot but not boiling.

Fruit Fool

This can be made from any of the stewed fruit bases described above.

Serves 4–6   300–450 calories in each serving

900 g (2 lb) fruit, stewed as described above: rhubarb or gooseberries are especially good
300 ml (½ pint) natural yogurt or cooker-top egg custard, (see page 194)

honey or sugar to taste
150 ml (6 fl oz) whipping cream

Puree the fruit in a food processor or liquidizer, or by pushing it through a nylon sieve. Or just mash it well. Mix the fruit with the yogurt or custard to make a thick, creamy mixture. Sweeten as necessary. Whisk the cream until it is softly peaking but not too stiff, then gently fold this into the fruit mixture. If you're using egg custard to make the fool, whisk the two egg whites which will be over until they are standing in peaks, then fold these into the fruit mixture after you've added the cream.

Fruit Meringue

This is delicious if it is cooked very slowly, so that the meringue dries out and becomes crisp. Make half these quantities for two people; for one person, use a quarter of the quantity of fruit and half the amount of meringue topping. Bake these smaller ones for about 1 hour.

Serves 4   300–400 calories in each serving

900 g (2 lb) fruit, stewed as described above: rhubarb or apples are especially good

2 eggs, separated
2 rounded tablespoons real demerara sugar

Set the oven to 150°C/300°F/Gas Mark 2. Mash the stewed fruit so that it has a smoothish texture, then add the egg yolks. Put the mixture into a shallow ovenproof casserole. Whisk the egg whites until they are stiff and glossy, then whisk in the sugar. Spoon this on top of the fruit, spreading it across the dish so that it reaches the edge all round and no fruit is visible. If you leave gaps, steam will come up from the fruit and the meringue won't get nice and crisp. Bake for 1–1½ hours, until the meringue is crisp and sounds hollow when you tap it lightly. Serve hot or cold.

BREAD BASE

Slices of bread, or breadcrumbs, have long been used to make economical puddings. Here are four traditional ones; they're cheap, filling and invariably popular.

Veiled Country Lass

This is a Danish pudding which consists of layers of crisp crumbs and apple puree. It's served cold with a topping of whipped cream (or natural yogurt, if you prefer).

Apple puree made as above from 900 g/2 lb cooking apples

Serves 4   550 calories in each serving

For the crumb layers:

50 g (2 oz) butter
12 heaped tablespoons soft
   wholemeal breadcrumbs
2 tablespoons demerara sugar
25 g (1 oz) plain chocolate,
   grated

½ teaspoon cinnamon
150 g (5 fl oz) whipping cream,
   whipped
2–3 tablespoons raspberry jam
   (optional)

To make crumb layer, melt the butter in a large saucepan or frying pan, add the crumbs and sugar and fry gently, stirring often, until the crumbs are brown and crisp. Remove from the heat and add the grated chocolate and cinnamon; stir until the chocolate has melted. Put a layer of crumbs into the bottom of serving bowl – a glass one is nice – then put a layer of apple on top of that. Continue in layers until all the apple and crumbs have been used, ending with crumbs. Cool, then chill. Just before you want to serve the pudding spread the cream or yogurt over the top and decorate, if you like, with some little dollops of raspberry jam.

Apple Charlotte

Another apple and crumb pudding, this time the British version, and served hot, with some cream or natural yogurt.

Serves 4   400 calories in each serving

*grated rind of 1 well-scrubbed
   lemon*

*apple puree made as above from
   900 g (2 lb) cooking apples*

For the crumbs:

*50 g (2 oz) butter
12 heaped tablespoons soft
   wholemeal breadcrumbs*

*2 tablespoons demerara sugar
¹/₂ teaspoon cinnamon*

Add the grated lemon rind to the apple puree. Set the oven to
190°C/375°F/Gas Mark 5. To make the crumb layer, melt the
butter in a large saucepan or frying pan, add the crumbs and sugar
and fry gently, stirring often, until the crumbs are brown and crisp.
Remove from the heat and add the cinnamon. Butter a fairly deep
ovenproof dish and sprinkle two thirds of the crumb mixture into
it, pressing it up the sides of the dish. Spoon the apple mixture in on
top and sprinkle with the remaining crumb mixture and the rest of
the sugar. Bake for 40–45 minutes, until golden brown and crisp.
Serve hot.

Summer Pudding

This traditional pudding can be made cheaply when red summer
fruit is in season; it's also good made with plums, when they're
cheap, later on in the summer, and also blackberries or bilberries.
You can make this any size you like; a mini one for one person,
using a quarter of these ingredients, or a half size, for two, works
equally well as a big one, but cut the bread thin, as there will be
more bread in proportion to fruit than with a larger pudding.

Serves 6   300 calories in each serving

225 g (8 oz) cooking apples,
  peeled and sliced
15 g (½ oz) butter
750–900 g (1½–2 lb) red fruit
  such as raspberries,
  redcurrants, blackcurrants,
  blackberries, strawberries,
  plums

sugar
about 8 slices of bread, crusts
  removed

Put the apples into a large saucepan with the butter and simmer gently, covered, for about 10 minutes, until the apples are tender. Then put in the red fruit (remove the stones from the plums first, if you're using these). Bring the mixture up to the boil and simmer gently until the red fruit is tender. Sweeten to taste. Remove from the heat. Grease a medium-sized pudding basin. Cut a piece of bread to fit over the base of the basin; dip the bread in the fruit mixture so that it soaks up the juice and becomes completely stained red, then press it into the bottom of the basin. (If there isn't enough juice to soak the bread, stir in a small cupful of boiling water.) Prepare the rest of the bread in the same way, cutting it to fit round the sides of the basin so that it is completely lined with bread (which can overlap a bit, but don't leave any gaps). Then spoon in the fruit, draining off the juice so that the pudding won't be too liquid. When the basin is full, cover the top with more soaked bread. Put a small plate or saucer on top of the pudding and stand a weight on top. Stand the bowl on a plate (to catch any drips which might overflow) and leave in the fridge or a cool place overnight. Next day, loosen the edges of the pudding with a palette knife and turn the pudding out. Some whipped cream or thick natural yogurt goes well with this.

Bread and Butter Pudding

These quantities can be doubled if you're serving four people; increase the cooking time to 45–50 minutes. Or halve them for one person (using 1 small egg) and cook for about 15–20 minutes.

Serves 2   380 calories in each serving

2 thin slices of stale bread,	*1 egg*
buttered, and crusts removed	*150 ml (5 fl oz) milk*
2 heaped tablespoons raisins or	*a little demerara sugar and*
sultanas	*butter to finish*

Set the oven to 170°C/325°F/Gas Mark 3. Cut the slices of bread into four. Layer the bread into a shallow ovenproof dish with the raisins or sultanas, ending with a layer of bread. Beat the egg with the milk and pour this over the bread. Sprinkle a little sugar on top and dot with a few pieces of butter. Bake for 30–40 minutes, until set.

SPONGE BASE

A sponge mixture is quickly made if you use the easy all-in-one method, and can form the basis of filling and popular family puddings. Here are two, a basic baked fruit sponge, and a basic steamed pudding.

Steamed Pudding

You can put jam or syrup into the base of the pudding basin, depending on your favourite, and serve the pudding with extra warmed jam or syrup. Yes, it's filling and fattening, but wonderful for a treat on a cold day. A mini one, for one person, made in a tiny basin or an old cup, works equally well, using a quarter of these quantities and half a beaten egg. Steam this for 40 minutes; a two person size needs steaming for about 1 hour.

Serves 4   600 calories in each serving

2 heaped tablespoons jam or
  syrup
4 heaped tablespoons 85%
  wholewheat self-raising flour

1 teaspoon baking powder
125 g (4 oz) soft butter
4 rounded tablespoons sugar
2 eggs

Grease a medium-sized pudding basin and put the jam or syrup into the base. Put the flour, baking powder, butter, sugar and eggs into a bowl and beat together for 1–2 minutes until thick, smooth and slightly glossy. Spoon the mixture into the bowl on top of the jam or syrup. Cover the basin with a piece of foil, tie with string and stand the bowl in a saucepan containing enough boiling water to come half way up the basin. Let the pudding simmer for 1½ hours. Keep an eye on the water level and top it up with more boiling water from the kettle if it gets too low. Remove the foil covering, slip a palette knife around the sides of the sponge and turn it out onto a warmed plate.

Fruit Sponge Pudding

This can be made with any fruit in season: cooking apples or pears, rhubarb, gooseberries or plums. You can spice up the mixture if you like by adding ½ teaspoonful of ground cinnamon or ginger to the fruit, or the grated rind of a well-scrubbed lemon or orange to the sponge. For two people, make a half quantity and bake for 30– 40 minutes; for one, use a quarter of the quantities (half a beaten egg) and bake for about 20 minutes.

Serves 4   620 calories in each serving

450 g (1 lb) cooking apples or
  pears, peeled, cored and sliced;
  or rhubarb, cut into chunks, or
  gooseberries, 'topped and
  tailed', or plums, halved and
  stones removed

1 tablespoon water
3 rounded tablespoons sugar

For the sponge topping

4 heaped tablespoons 85%
  wholewheat self-raising flour
1 teaspoon baking powder

125 g (4 oz) soft butter
4 rounded tablespoons sugar
2 eggs

Set oven to 180°C/350°F/Gas Mark 4. Grease a medium-sized baking dish and put the fruit into it; sprinkle with the sugar and water. Put the flour, baking powder, butter, sugar and eggs into a bowl and beat together for 1–2 minutes until thick, smooth and slightly glossy. Spoon the mixture on top of the fruit and spread evenly. Bake for 45–60 minutes, until the fruit is soft when pierced with a skewer and the sponge springs back when touched lightly in the centre.

CRUMBLES

Fruit Crumble

A fruit crumble is always popular and is easy to make. Apples and hard pears need to be cooked first, as described on page 177–78, but this isn't necessary for most other fruits. Rhubarb, plums, soft sweet pears, gooseberries, bilberries and blackcurrants can be put straight into the dish, making these quick crumbles to prepare. Use half or a third of these ingredients to make a crumble for two people and bake for 20–30 minutes; for one person use 175 g (6 oz) of fruit and a level tablespoon of sugar, 2 heaped and 1 level tablespoon flour, 40 g (1½ oz) butter and 1 heaped and 1 level tablespoonful of sugar for the crumble. Bake this for about 20 minutes.

Serves 6   650 calories in each serving

900 g (2 lb) of your chosen fruit   3 rounded tablespoons sugar
  – rhubarb cut into chunks,
  plums, halved and stones
  removed, gooseberries,
  topped and tailed, bilberries
  or blackcurrants, stalks
  removed

For the crumble

9 heaped tablespoons self-   175 g (6 oz) butter
  raising 85% wholewheat   6 rounded tablespoons
  flour   demerara sugar

Set the oven to 200°C/400°F/Gas Mark 6. Put the fruit into a lightly-greased large shallow ovenproof dish, add the sugar and mix gently; see that the fruit is in an even layer. Put the flour into a bowl and rub in the butter with your fingertips until the mixture looks like fine breadcrumbs and there are no obvious bits of fat showing. Then add the sugar and mix gently. Spoon the crumble topping over the fruit in an even layer, covering all the fruit. Bake the crumble for 30–40 minutes, until the crumble is crisp and lightly browned and the fruit feels tender when pierced with a skewer.

FLANS AND TARTS

Strawberry Tart

A luscious shiny red tart is one of the best things to make from summer strawberries or other red fruit, such as redcurrants, glazed with a toning jam or jelly.

Serves 4–6   250–370 calories in each serving

4 heaped tablespoons self-
raising 85% wholewheat
flour

65 g (2½ oz) butter or
polyunsaturated margarine

For the filling

350–450 g (12 oz – 1 lb)
strawberries

4 heaped tablespoons
strawberry jam

Set the oven to 200°C/400°F/Gas Mark 6. Lightly grease a 20 cm (8 inch) flan tin or other suitable dish. To make the pastry, put the flour into a bowl with ½ teaspoonful of salt and rub in the fat with your fingertips until the mixture looks like fine breadcrumbs. Press the mixture together to make a dough – as the proportion of fat is a little higher than usual, you shouldn't need to add any water. Roll the pastry out and slide it into the flan tin; trim the edges. Prick the base of the flan case and bake for 20 minutes, until the pastry feels firm and crisp to a light touch. Remove from the oven and cool. Wash the strawberries and halve them if they're large. Arrange the strawberries in the flan case. Melt the jam gently in a small saucepan and pour over the top of the strawberries. Cool.

Jam or Lemon Curd Tart

This is a more economical version of the above, and particularly good if you can use homemade plum jam or lemon curd. Make the pastry case as described above, but spoon the jam into it before baking. There is no need to melt the jam first. For an extra special, extravagant version, whisk a small carton of whipping cream until it's standing in soft peaks, spoon this on top of the tart when it has cooled and top with a little coarsely grated chocolate or some toasted flaked almonds.

Treacle Tart

You could replace some of the syrup with black treacle if you prefer.

Serves 4–6   280–420 calories in each serving

For the pastry:

125 g (4 oz) (4 heaped   65 g (2½ oz) *butter or*
   tablespoons) self-raising 85%   *polyunsaturated margarine*
   wholewheat flour

For the filling:

6 tablespoons golden syrup   1 teaspoon lemon juice
3 slices wholewheat bread,
   made into crumbs

First make the pastry; put the flour into a bowl with ½ teaspoonful of salt and rub in the fat with your fingertips until the mixture looks like fine breadcrumbs. Press the mixture together to make a dough – as the proportion of fat is a little higher than usual, you shouldn't need to add any water. Set the oven to 200°C/400°F/Gas Mark 6. Roll out the pastry and line a 20 cm (8 inch) flan dish; trim the edges. Roll the trimmings into strips to make a lattice on top of the tart, keep on one side. Chill the flan case and pastry strips while you make the filling. Put the golden syrup into a saucepan and heat gently to melt, then remove from the heat and add the crumbs and lemon juice. Spoon this mixture into the flan case, level the surface, arrange the strips in a lattice on top. Bake for 25 minutes, until the pastry is crisp and lightly browned. Serve warm.

Top-Crust Apple Pie

Wholewheat flour gives this traditional pie a deliciously nutty flavour. Other fruits such as blackberries (or a mixture of blackberries and apples), rhubarb, pears, gooseberries or plums can be used: just prepare them as described on pages 177–78 and use them in place of the apples. If the fruit is very sharp (as are gooseberries, rhubarb or some plums, allow more sugar – 4–6 rounded tablespoons). To make a smaller pie, for one or two people, use a third of these quantities and make the pie in a small dish; bake for 15–20 minutes.

Serves 6   300 calories in each serving

6 heaped tablespoons plain
   wholewheat flour, 85% or
   100%

75 g (3 oz) butter
6 teaspoons cold water

For the filling:

750 g (1½ lb) cooking apples,
   peeled, cored and sliced

3 rounded tablespoons soft
   brown sugar

To finish:

milk to glaze

Set the oven to 200°C/400°F/Gas Mark 6. Sift the flour into a bowl, adding the bran left behind in the sieve, too. Rub in the butter until the mixture looks like breadcrumbs, then add the water to make a dough. Roll out the pastry and cut it to fit the dish with about 1 cm (½ inch) over all round. Cut another strip or strips about 1 cm (½ inch) wide and long enough to go round the rim of the pie dish. Put the fruit into the pie dish and sprinkle in the sugar. Brush the rim of the pie dish with water and press the pastry strip on to it. Ease the pastry on top of the pie, resting on the strip of pastry round the rim. Trim the edges. Make a steam-hole in the centre of the pie. Brush the top with milk. Bake for about 30 minutes, until the pastry is crisp and lightly browned.

Double-Crust Fruit Pie

Any of the stewed fruit mixtures can be used as a filling for this pie; prepare and cool them in advance. To make a pie for one or two people, use a third of these ingredients and a deep ovenproof saucer to bake the pie.

Serves 6   400 calories in each serving

8 heaped tablespoons plain
   wholewheat flour, 85% or
   100%

125 g (4 oz) butter
3 tablespoons cold water

For the filling:

1 quantity of stewed fruit (see
   pages 177–78) prepared and
   cooled

To finish:

milk to glaze

Set the oven to 200°C/400°F/Gas Mark 6. Make the pastry as described above. Roll out just over half the pastry on a floured board and use to line a 20–22 cm (8–9 inch) pie plate. Spoon the fruit on top of the pastry to within 1 cm (½ inch) of the edges. Roll the rest of the pastry and put over the top of the fruit. Trim, decorate and make two or three steam holes. Brush with milk. Bake for about 30 minutes, until the pastry is crisp and lightly browned.

YOGURT BASE

Yogurt is a healthy and convenient food and can be made into a number of delicious puddings, as well as being useful as topping, instead of cream, and, with seasoning and chopped herbs, as a savoury sauce or salad dressing.

How to make your own yogurt

If you like yogurt, you can save a lot of money by making your own and it only takes about 5 minutes of preparation. All you need is a wide-necked vacuum flask (the cheapest kind will do) which will hold a pint of liquid, and a teaspoonful of plain yogurt – choose one made from 'live' yogurt from a health shop or supermarket. Bring a pint of milk to the boil, then leave it to stand until you can comfortably dip your little finger into it. Whisk in the skin from the top of the milk together with 2 heaped tablespoons of skimmed milk powder and a teaspoonful of the yogurt. Scald the vacuum flask to sterilize it by filling it with boiling water then tipping it out. Pour the milk mixture into the vacuum, screw on the lid and leave it overnight or for 10–12 hours. Then when you open it you should find perfect, thick yogurt. Save a bit of this for starting off your next batch. Keep the yogurt in the fridge, and it will get even thicker.

You can make the yogurt from any kind of milk – use skimmed milk if you want to reduce the calories. When you leave the mixture to stand, make sure you put the vacuum in a place where nobody will touch it, and don't open it for 10 hours or so, because for some reason knocks and rough movements can upset the fermentation process. You may find you need to buy a new tub of starter yogurt from time to time – if the finished mixture does not get as thick as usual.

Fruit Yogurt

You can make this by adding some chopped fresh fruit to your plain yogurt and some honey or sugar to taste. Or you can use a good fruity jam, without colouring or preservatives, or your own make, if you have any. The reduced sugar jams which you can buy are excellent stirred into yogurt. They're expensive, but you don't need much.

Strained Yogurt

If you want to make your yogurt gloriously thick and rich-tasting, like Greek yogurt, all you do is put a large sieve or colander over a bowl and line the sieve or colander with clean gauze (from the chemist). Scald the gauze by pouring a kettleful of boiling water through it, then tip the yogurt into the sieve or colander and leave it to drip overnight. Then turn the yogurt into a bowl and keep covered in the fridge or a cold place. It's lovely as a thick topping for fruit salads, or just as it is, with some clear honey spooned over it. You can add other embellishments such as a few fresh, chopped walnuts or other nuts and some dried fruits – sultanas which you have plumped by a soak in boiling water for 15 minutes are good. For real indulgence, try your strained yogurt with some fresh dates, a drizzle of good clear honey and a spoonful of thick cream!

EGG CUSTARD BASE

Real egg custard is delicious and nourishing as a pudding. It also makes an excellent base for a quick homemade ice cream or can be made into a quick and easy trifle. There are two types of egg custard, the kind you make in a saucepan on top of the cooker, and oven-baked egg custard.

Oven-Baked Egg Custard

For each person allow 1 egg, whisked and made up to 150 ml (¼ pint) with milk, and a rounded teaspoonful of sugar. If you keep a jar of caster sugar with a vanilla pod in it for making this kind of delicately-flavoured dish, this will flavour the custard; otherwise add a drop or two of real vanilla essence too. Whisk all your ingredients together, pour the mixture into a suitable ovenproof container – a small ramekin for one person – stand the dish in a baking tray and pour hot water into the tin so that it reaches half way up the basin. Bake at 180°C/350°F/Gas Mark 4 until the custard has set and a knife blade inserted in the centre comes out clean. This will take about 40–60 minutes. The custard can be served hot or it can be cooled then chilled before serving, which gives it a thicker, creamier texture. A little fresh nutmeg grated over the top of the custard before baking is pleasant.

Caramel Custard

To make this, for each person put a rounded tablespoonful of granulated sugar into a saucepan and heat until it melts and is golden brown. Remove from the heat immediately, stand back and add, again for each serving, a teaspoonful of water. This will melt the caramel; stir it to make it smooth, then pour it into an ovenproof dish, such as, for one, a small ramekin, tipping the dish so that the caramel coats the base. Make the custard as described above and pour this on top of the caramel. Cook the custard as described above. Cool then chill the custard, then loosen the edges by slipping the blade of a knife round, invert the dish over a serving plate and turn out the custard.

Cooker-Top Egg Custard

If you start this off with a little cornflour, it makes the custard easier to make without curdling. Put two egg yolks into a bowl and blend to a smooth cream with a heaped teaspoonful of cornflour and a little milk taken from 600 ml (1 pint). Heat the rest of the milk to boiling-point in a medium-sized saucepan, then pour it over the cornflour mixture, stir, and tip the whole mixture into the saucepan. Stir over the heat until the mixture thickens, then let it come to the boil, boil for 30 seconds only, to cook the cornflour, then remove from the heat immediately. Stir in a heaped tablespoonful of vanilla sugar if you have it, or caster sugar and a few drops of real vanilla essence. This can be served hot or cold.

Trifle

To make a good trifle, put some homemade jam sandwich sponge, broken into bite-sized pieces, into the base of a serving dish. Sprinkle this with a little sherry or sweet wine if you like, or moisten with some orange juice. Then pour a cooker-top egg custard over the sponge and leave to cool. After that, cover the whole of the surface with some whipped whipping cream and some toasted flaked almonds, if you like.

Ice Cream

You can use a batch of cooker-top custard as a base for this, or you can also use up left-over oven-baked custard, if you have any. Just fold an equal quantity of whipping cream, lightly whipped, into the cold custard. Pour the mixture into a polythene container and freeze until the ice cream is getting firm around the edges, then give it a good whisking and put it back to finish freezing. Let the ice cream stand at room temperature for about 30 minutes before serving, then beat it a bit before putting it out onto the plates to make it nice and smooth. Another wonderful way of making ice cream is to mix 350 g (12 oz) sieved, pureed fruit with 300 ml (½ pint) whipping cream and enough sugar to taste. Or, for the simplest ice cream of all, rich, creamy, sweet and unfailingly popular, whip together a small can (225 g (8 oz) size) of condensed milk and 300 ml (½ pint) of whipping cream – this one is nice served with a sharp sauce made from pureed redcurrants or blackcurrants, slightly sweetened.

CHEESECAKES

Finally, here are two very easy recipes for cheesecakes, one cooked and one uncooked.

Cheesecake (uncooked)

This is a not too expensive special occasion pudding that's very easy to make. Quark is a very low fat soft white cheese which makes up for the fat in the double cream which is necessary to give the mixture body.

Serves 6   420 calories in each serving

125 g (4 oz) wholemeal biscuits,
   crushed
50 g (2 oz) melted butter
400 g (14 oz) Quark or low-fat
   soft white cheese

150 ml (5 fl oz) double cream
3–4 tablespoons sugar

For the topping

225 g (8 oz) strawberries
2–3 tablespoons strawberry or
   redcurrant jam, melted

Mix together the biscuit crumbs and butter; press mixture into the base of a 20 cm (8 inch) spring-form flan tin or other suitable shallow dish. Put the Quark, cream and sugar into a bowl and whisk together until thick; spoon mixture on top of the biscuit mixture and level off. Wash and half the strawberries; arrange on top of the white cheese mixture. Pour the jam over the top of the strawberries. Chill before serving.

Uncooked Cheesecake For One Person

Crush two digestive biscuits and mix with a tablespoonful of melted butter; press into a small ramekin or individual-sized shallow flan dish. Beat together 50 g (2 oz) curd cheese or skimmed milk soft white cheese and 2 tablespoons of whipping cream, until mixture holds its shape. Add a heaped teaspoonful of sugar. Spread the mixture on top of the biscuit mixture. Arrange 50–125 g (2–4 oz) strawberries on top, then spoon 1–2 tablespoons melted redcurrant jelly over the strawberries and leave to cool.

Cheesecake (Cooked)

This is an easy and economical cheesecake. In the winter it is good topped with alternating circles of halved and seeded purple and green grapes, and melted apricot jam, instead of the strawberries. For one or two people, make a half quantity (use a whole egg) using a 12 cm (6 inch) flan dish, and baking for 15–20 minutes.

Serves 6   300 calories in each serving

*125 g (4 oz) wholemeal biscuits,
    crushed
50 g (2 oz) melted butter
225 g (8 oz) curd cheese
2 tablespoons sugar*

*1 egg, beaten
1 tablespoon lemon juice
a few drops of real vanilla
    essence*

For the topping

*225 g (8 oz) strawberries
2–3 tablespoons strawberry or
    redcurrant jam, melted*

Set the oven to 190°C/375°F/Gas Mark 5. Mix together the biscuit crumbs and butter; press mixture into the base of a 20 cm (8 inch) flan tin or other suitable shallow dish. Put the curd cheese and sugar into a bowl with the egg, lemon juice and vanilla and beat together until smooth. Pour the mixture on top of the biscuit mixture. Bake for about 20 minutes until set in the middle. Turn off the oven and leave the cheesecake to cool in the oven: if it cools too quickly, it may crack. To finish wash and half the strawberries and arrange on top of the cheesecake. Pour the jam over the top of the strawberries. Chill before serving.

17 Express Bakery

Making your own cakes not only saves money, but also enables you to know exactly what is going into them, and to use the best and healthiest ingredients. They needn't be very time-consuming to make: here are some very simple suggestions.

BASIC RUBBING-IN METHOD

This easy method involves first rubbing the fat into the flour with your fingertips, then adding other ingredients.

Easy Wholewheat Scones

These can be whizzed up in no time and are delicious for a quick tea-time treat, especially with some jam and cream, or reduced-sugar jam and thick yogurt if you're feeling more virtuous!

Makes 6–8   160–220 calories in each serving

225 g (8 oz) (8 heaped
  tablespoons) self-raising 85%
  wholewheat flour
2 teaspoons baking powder
50 g (2 oz) butter or margarine
1 egg, whisked and made up to
  150 ml (¼ pint) with 2
  tablespoons milk

Set the oven to 220°C/425°F/Gas Mark 7. Sift the flour and baking powder into a bowl, then add the butter and rub in with your fingertips. Add the egg and milk mixture and mix to a soft but not sticky dough. Turn this out onto a floured board and knead lightly, then press out to a depth of at least 1 cm (½ inch), so that the scones are nice and high when they're cooked. Cut the scones out with a 5 cm (2 inch) round cutter and place them on a floured baking sheet. Bake the scones for 12–15 minutes, until they're golden brown and the sides spring back when lightly pressed. Cool on a wire rack, or serve immediately.

Cheese Scones

These are delicious to eat warm from the oven, for a quick lunch or supper. They're good buttered, with a little salad, with some fresh firm tomatoes and crisp celery stick.

Makes 6–8   180–240 calories in each serving

225 g (8 oz) (8 heaped
   tablespoons) self-raising 85%
   wholewheat flour
½ *teaspoon dry mustard*
2 *teaspoons baking powder*

25 g (1 oz) *butter or margarine*
1 *egg, whisked and made up to*
   150 ml (¼ *pint) with 2*
   tablespoons milk
75 g (3 oz) *grated cheese*

Set the oven to 220°C/425°F/Gas Mark 7. Sift the flour, mustard powder and baking powder into a bowl, then add the butter and rub in with your fingertips. Add the egg and milk mixture and half the grated cheese and mix to a soft but not sticky dough. Turn this out onto a floured board and knead lightly, then press out to a depth of at least 1 cm/½ inch, so that the scones are nice and high when they're cooked. Cut the scones out with a 5 cm (2 inch) round cutter and place them on a floured baking sheet. Sprinkle the rest of the grated cheese on top of the scones, then bake them for 12–15 minutes, until they're golden brown and the sides spring back when lightly pressed. Cool on a wire rack, or serve immediately.

Wholewheat Jam Tarts

Children love this wholefood version of an old favourite and they make useful lunch box treats.

Makes 12   90 calories in each serving

125 g (4 oz) (4 heaped
   tablespoons) plain 100%
   wholewheat flour

50 g (2 oz) *butter*
6 *teaspoons cold water*

For the filling:

4 *heaped tablespoons jam,*
   preferably reduced-sugar type

Set the oven to 190°C/375°F/Gas Mark 5. Grease a shallow bun tin. Put the flour into a bowl; add the butter and rub in with your fingertips until the mixture looks like breadcrumbs. Add the water, then press the mixture together to form a dough. Roll the pastry out carefully on a lightly-floured board, then cut into 12 circles using a 6 cm (2½ inch) cutter. Press a pastry circle lightly into each bun cavity, then put a heaped teaspoonful of jam onto each. Bake the jam tarts towards the top of the oven for about 10 minutes, until the pastry is lightly browned. Cool in the tin.

Date Fingers

These crisp fingers rely on the dates for sweetness, with no added sugar.

Makes 12–16   140–190 calories in each serving

225 g (8 oz) (8 heaped   125 g (4 oz) butter
   tablespoons) self-raising 85%   3 tablespoons cold water
   or 100% wholewheat flour

For the filling

225 g (8 oz) dates (not   150 ml (¼ pint) water
   sugar-rolled)

Set the oven to 200°C/400°F/Gas Mark 6. First prepare the filling; put the dates and water into a small saucepan and cook gently for 5–10 minutes until the dates are soft. Mash the dates, making sure that there are no hard pieces of stem or stone amongst them. Leave to cool. To make the pastry, put the wholewheat flour into a bowl with ½ teaspoonful of salt and rub in the fat with your fingertips until the mixture looks like fine breadcrumbs. Add the water, then press the mixture together to make a dough. Divide the mixture in half. Roll out half to fit a swiss roll tin (or just roll it into an oblong roughly this size and place on a baking sheet if you prefer). Spread the date mixture on top of the pastry. Roll out the rest of the pastry to fit the top, press into position and trim the edges. Prick all over with a fork. Bake for 30 minutes, until pastry is firm and lightly browned. Cool for 30 minutes in the tin, then cut into fingers, ease out of the tin and place on a wire rack to finish cooling.

Quick and Easy Fruit Cake

This cake made without eggs will keep for 7–10 days in a tin.

Makes one 20 cm round cake   *15,600 calories in whole cake*

350 g (12 oz) (12 heaped
    tablespoons) 85% or 100%
    plain wholewheat flour
1 teaspoon mixed spice
175 g (6 oz) butter
6 oz rounded tablespoons real
    barbados sugar
225 g (8 oz) mixed dried fruit
125 g (4 oz) glace cherries,
    rinsed and halved (optional)

grated rind of 1 well-scrubbed
    orange
1 heaped tablespoon ground
    almonds (optional)
125 ml (4 fl oz) milk
2 tablespoons vinegar
3/4 teaspoon bicarbonate of
    soda

Set the oven to 150°C/300°F/Gas Mark 2. Grease a 20 cm (8 inch) cake tin and line with a double layer of greased greaseproof paper. Sift the flour and spice into a bowl, adding the bran from the sieve, too, if you're using 100% wholewheat flour. Rub the butter into the flour with your fingers until the mixture resembles breadcrumbs, then add the dried fruit, cherries, orange rind and ground almonds. Warm half the milk in a small saucepan and add the vinegar. Dissolve the bicarbonate of soda in the rest of the milk, then add to the milk and vinegar mixture. Quickly stir this into the flour and fruit, mixing well so that everything is combined. Spoon mixture into prepared cake tin. Bake for 2–2½ hours, until a skewer inserted into the centre of the cake comes out clean. Leave the cake in the tin to cool, then strip off the greaseproof paper.

Rock Cakes

Easy to make, spicy and delicious eaten while still warm.

Makes 8   300 calories in each serving

225 g (8 oz) (8 heaped
  tablespoons) self-raising
  wholewheat flour
½ teaspoon mixed spice
125 g (4 oz) butter

3 rounded tablespoons
  demerara sugar
125 g (4 oz) mixed dried fruit
1 egg, beaten with 1 tablespoon
  milk

Set the oven to 200°C/400°F/Gas Mark 6. Sift the flour and spice into a bowl, then rub in the butter with your fingertips until the mixture looks like fine breadcrumbs. Add two thirds of the sugar, the fruit and egg and milk mixture, and mix lightly, so that the mixture just holds together. Put heaps of the mixture onto a greased baking sheet or tin, leaving a little room around for spreading, then sprinkle with the rest of the sugar. Bake for about 15 minutes, until lightly browned. Cool on a wire rack.

MELTING METHOD

Another beautifully easy method for cake making, where the fat, sugar and any syrups are melted together before adding the dry ingredients. The important point to remember with this method is to let the melted mixture cool down before adding the rest of the ingredients – the pan should be cool enough to touch. If you have a microwave, you can make things even easier for yourself by putting the ingredients to be melted into a large mixing bowl, microwaving until melted, then leaving to cool, before adding the rest of the ingredients to the same bowl.

Flapjacks

One of the quickest recipes ever and popular with everyone.

Makes 12–16   130–170 calories in each serving

100 g (4 oz) butter
6 rounded tablespoons real
*   barbados sugar*

1 slightly round tablespoon
*   golden syrup*
175 g (6 oz) (8 rounded
*   tablespoons) rolled oats*

Set oven to 190°C/375°F/Gas Mark 5. Grease a 7 × 11 inch Swiss roll tin. Put the butter, sugar and syrup into a large saucepan and heat gently until melted, then remove from the heat and stir in the oats. Mix well, then spread the mixture into the tin and press down evenly. Bake for 20 minutes, until brown all over. Mark into fingers while still hot, then leave in the tin until cold. The flapjacks become crisp as they cool and keep well in an airtight tin.

Parkin

Nice and easy, and quite nourishing too, this parkin gets stickier if wrapped in foil and stored in a tin for 2–7 days.

Makes 12 slices   170 calories in each serving

125 g (4 oz) (4 heaped
*   tablespoons) plain 100%*
*   wholewheat flour*
2 teaspoons baking powder
2 teaspoons ground ginger
125 g (4 oz) (4 heaped
*   tablespoons) medium*
*   oatmeal*

3 rounded tablespoons real
*   barbados sugar*
2 heaped tablespoons black
*   treacle*
2 heaped tablespoons golden
*   syrup*
125 g (4 oz) butter
175 ml (6 fl oz) milk

Set the oven to 180°C/350°F/Gas Mark 4. Line a 20 cm (8 inch) square tin with greased greaseproof paper. Sift the flour, baking powder and ginger into a bowl, adding the residue of bran from the sieve, as well, and also the oatmeal. Put the sugar, treacle, golden syrup and butter into a saucepan and heat gently until melted. Cool until you can comfortably put your hand against the pan, then add the milk. Add to the dry ingredients, mixing well. Pour the mixture into the prepared tin. Bake for 50–60 minutes, until firm to the touch. Lift the parkin out of the tin and put on a wire tray to cool, then cut into pieces. Makes 12–16 pieces.

Gingerbread

This gingerbread gets sticky if you wrap it in foil and store it in a tin, for several days. It will keep well in a tin for 7–14 days.

Makes 12 pieces   250 calories in each serving

1 heaped tablespoonful golden syrup
6 heaped tablespoons black treacle
3 rounded tablespoons real barbados sugar
125 g (4 oz) butter
225 g (8 oz) (8 heaped tablespoons) plain 100% wholewheat flour
2 teaspoons baking powder
½ teaspoon ground ginger
2 eggs, beaten
½ teaspoon bicarbonate of soda
150 ml (5 fl oz) milk

Set the oven to 160°C/325°F/Gas Mark 3. Grease a 20 cm (8 inch) square tin and line with greased greaseproof paper. Melt the golden syrup, treacle, sugar and butter in a saucepan over a gentle heat. Cool. Sift the flour, ginger and baking powder into a bowl, adding the residue of bran from the sieve, too. Make a well in the centre and pour in the treacle mixture and the beaten eggs. Dissolve the bicarbonate of soda in the milk, then stir this into the mixture. Pour the mixture into the tin. Bake for 1½ hours, until well-risen and firm to touch. Cool in the tin, then strip off the paper and cut into slices.

CREAMED MIXTURES

These creamed mixtures can be very simple to make if you use the 'all-in-one' method, and the results are excellent every time.

All-in-one Sponge

A lovely light cake that couldn't be easier to make.

Makes one 20 cm (8 inch) cake   *2200 calories in whole cake*

125 g (4 oz) (4 heaped tablespoons) self-raising 85% wholewheat flour
1 teaspoon baking powder
125 g (4 oz) (4 rounded tablespoons) light brown sugar

125 g (4 oz) soft butter or polyunsaturated margarine
2 eggs

For the filling and topping

3 tablespoons warmed jam, preferably reduced sugar type

a little caster sugar to sprinkle on top

Set the oven to 170°C/325°F/Gas Mark 3. Grease two 18 cm (7 inch) sandwich tins with butter, then line the base of each with a circle of greased greaseproof paper. Sift the flour and baking powder into a bowl, add the sugar, fat and eggs. Beat with a wooden spoon for 2 minutes, until the mixture is smooth, thick and glossy. Spoon the mixture into the prepared tin, scraping round the edge of the bowl with a spatula. Level the top. Bake, without opening the oven door, for 30 minutes. Test whether the cakes are done by pressing them lightly in the centre with a fingertip; if the sponge bounces back afterwards, it's done. Leave the cakes in the tin to cool for 1 minute, then turn them out onto a wire rack, carefully remove the greaseproof paper, then leave the cakes to cool completely. Sandwich the cakes together with jam and sprinkle with caster sugar.

Iced Fingers

Made from the same mixture, this is very popular and easy to make.

Makes 12–16 slices   150–200 calories in each serving

125 g (4 oz) (4 heaped
   tablespoons) self-raising 85%
   wholewheat flour
1 teaspoon baking powder
125 g (4 oz) (4 rounded
   tablespoons) light brown
   sugar

125 g (4 oz) soft butter or
   polyunsaturated margarine
2 eggs

For the icing.

4 heaped tablespoons icing
   sugar

1–2 tablespoons water

Set the oven to 170°C/325°F/Gas Mark 3. Grease and line an 11 × 7 inch shallow tin. Sift the flour and baking powder into a bowl, add the sugar, fat and eggs. Beat with a wooden spoon for 2 minutes, until the mixture is smooth, thick and glossy. Spoon the mixture into the prepared tin, scraping round the edge of the bowl with a spatula. Level the top. Bake, without opening the oven door, for 30 minutes. Test whether the cakes are done by pressing them lightly in the centre with a fingertip; if the sponge bounces back afterwards, it's done. Leave to cool in the tin while you make the icing. Put the icing sugar into a bowl and beat in the water a little at a time until you have a thick mixture. Spread the icing over the top of the sponge then lift the whole thing out of the tin, using the paper to pick it up, and place on a wire rack. Cut into sections when cold. You can decorate the pieces with chopped nuts, sugar strands or a piece of glace cherry, if liked.

Fruit and Almond Fingers

For a delicious variation, add 125 g (4 oz) mixed dried fruit or chopped dates to the basic mixture and sprinkle 25–50 g (1–2 oz) flaked almonds on top before baking. This does not need icing.

Carob or Chocolate Fingers

Replace a tablespoonful of flour with the same amount of carob or cocoa powder and add a teaspoonful of vanilla extract to the mixture. Ice with melted chocolate or carob bar; or make icing as described, substituting 2 teaspoons of icing sugar for the same amount of carob or cocoa powder.

Carrot Cake

Add 2 grated carrots to the mixture, the grated rind of a well-scrubbed orange, 2 tablespoons chopped walnuts and 50–125 g (2–4 oz) sultanas to the mixture. Make an icing by blending together 75 g (3 oz) curd cheese, a tablespoonful of icing sugar and 25 g (1 oz) butter.

Orange Slices

Add the finely grated rind of a well-scrubbed orange to the mixture. Use orange juice to mix the icing instead of water.

Quick Buns

Makes 12   220 calories in each bun

175 g (6 oz) (6 heaped
    tablespoons) 85% or 100%
    wholewheat self-raising flour

125 g (4 oz) soft butter
4 rounded tablespoons sugar
2 eggs

For the icing .

4 heaped tablespoons icing
    sugar
1–2 tablespoons water

chopped nuts, or a few
    chocolate sugar strands or
    sliced glace cherries

Set the oven to 190°C/375°F/Gas Mark 5. Thoroughly grease a bun
tin. Sift the flour into a bowl, adding the bran from the sieve, too, if
you're using 100% wholewheat flour, then put in the butter, sugar
and eggs and beat well with a wooden spoon or with an electric
mixer, until all the ingredients are well-blended and the mixture is
thick and slightly glossy-looking. Drop a good heaped teaspoonful
of mixture into each section of the bun tin. Bake for 15–20 minutes
until the cakes have risen and feel firm to a light touch. Let the buns
cool for a couple of minutes, then ease them out of the tin with a
knife and leave them to cool on a wire tray.

  To make the icing, put the icing sugar into a bowl and beat in the
water a little at a time until you have a thick mixture. Spread a little
icing on top of each bun and decorate with some chopped nuts,
sugar strands or a piece of glace cherry.

Easy Shortbread

Makes a circle cutting into 12 pieces   220 calories in each serving

175 g (6 oz) butter
75 g (3 oz) soft brown sugar

250 g (9 oz) 85% wholewheat
    flour

209

Set the oven to 150°C/300°F/Gas Mark 2. Put the butter and sugar into a bowl and cream together until the sugar is blended, then add the flour and mix together to form a dough. Put the dough onto a floured surface, kneading it slightly. Then press it into a 20 cm (8 inch) flan tin, prick the top, and bake for 1¼–1½ hours until set and just beginning to go golden. Mark into sections with a knife, then leave to cool in the tin.

To make shortbread biscuits, roll the mixture out about 3 mm (⅛ inch) thick, cut into circles, place on a baking sheet and bake for about 30 minutes.

QUICK AND EASY BREADS

Wholewheat Bread

This is a very quick bread to make as it doesn't have any kneading.

Makes two 450 g (1 lb) loaves   70 calories in a 25 g (1 oz) slice

*450 g (1 lb) 100% wholewheat
  flour
2 level teaspoons salt
1 packet instant dried yeast*

*1 tablespoon honey, molasses or
  black treacle
about 350 ml (12 fl oz) tepid
  water*

Grease two 450 g (1 lb) bread tins thoroughly with butter. Put the flour, salt and yeast into a large bowl. Mix together the honey, molasses or treacle and the water; stir well, then add this to the flour. Mix well to make a dough that is just too soft to knead. Divide the dough in half and place one half in each tin. Cover tins loosely with clingfilm and leave in a warm place – or on the kitchen working surface – until the dough has risen by one third. This will take 30–45 minutes, depending on temperature. Fifteen minutes or so before the bread is ready, set oven to 230°C/450°F/Gas Mark 8. Bake the loaves for 35 minutes. Turn the loaves out of their tins and put them on a wire tray to cool.

18 Microwave Know-How

Using the microwave oven for normal cooking (rather than just for heating up dishes) saves time, and many of the recipes in this book can be speedily made in this way. If you are thinking of buying a microwave, I think that the ones which include a conventional grill and oven are well worth the extra money, because they give you the speed of the microwave with the brown and crisp results of traditional cooking. Also, in my opinion, you do not need a large variety of different power settings; these are only confusing. My microwave has just got full power (600 watts) and de-frost (230 watts) and I have found that quite sufficient for everything. Timings given in this section are for a 600 watt oven. For a 500 watt oven, increase the timings by approx 25 seconds for each minute.

For a 700 watt oven, decrease the timings by approximately 25 seconds for each minute.

Notes on using a microwave

Do not use any metal containers, or containers with a metal decoration; glass, tough plastic and ceramic containers are suitable.

Instead of covering with foil (which is not recommended for use in microwaves) use a plate or a transparent plastic film recommended as suitable for microwave ovens: read the packets. Many of the dishes need time to stand, after microwaving, to finish cooking; allow time for this.

NOTES ON MICROWAVING RECIPES IN THIS BOOK

SOUPS

Most of the soups in this book begin by frying an onion and other vegetables in butter. This can be done cleanly and easily in the microwave: put the vegetables and butter into a large bowl, cover with plastic film, pierce twice and microwave on full power for 5 minutes, stirring twice. Then add the water, re-cover and microwave on full power for 10 minutes, or until the vegetables are tender. Complete the soup as described in the recipe, pureeing as necessary and seasoning with salt and pepper.

Pistou, page 23: Put the onion and oil into a bowl, cover with plastic film, pierce two or three times, then microwave on full power for 2 minutes, stirring once. Then add the beans, vegetables, garlic, seasoning and dried basil, re-cover and cook for 2 minutes, stirring once. Then add the stock, re-cover and microwave on full power for 10 minutes, until all the vegetables are tender. Then add the pasta, re-cover and microwave on full power for 8 minutes, until the pasta is tender. Allow the soup to stand for 10 minutes, then season and serve.

Root Vegetable Soup, page 24: Simply put all the ingredients into a large bowl, cover with plastic film, pierce twice and microwave on full power for 10 minutes, stirring twice. Then allow to stand for 10 minutes before finishing the soup as described in the recipe.

Sauces

Sauces can be made speedily in the microwave, with no sticky pan to wash up afterwards.

Béchamel Sauce, page 27: Put 600 ml (1 pint) of milk into a bowl or jug with the small scraped carrot, piece of onion, bay leaf and 6 peppercorns. Microwave, uncovered, on full power, for 2–3 minutes, until the milk boils, then remove from the microwave, cover and leave on one side for 15 minutes; strain, and discard the carrot, onion and herbs and spices. Put the butter or margarine into a bowl or deep jug and microwave on full power for 1–2 minutes, until melted. Then stir in the flour and microwave for 1 minute, to cook slightly. Stir in the strained milk, return to the microwave and cook for 4–5 minutes, on full power, until thickened, stirring every minute or so to remove lumps and produce a smooth sauce. Other ingredients, such as chopped parsley, mushrooms or grated cheese can be added to the sauce at this point, as described in the recipes on page 28.

Tomato Sauce, page 28: Put the peeled and chopped onion into a bowl with 1 tablespoon of oil, cover with plastic film, pierce two or three times, then microwave on full power for 4 minutes, stirring twice. Then add the garlic clove and tomatoes, re-cover, and microwave for 2 minutes, stirring once. Complete as described on page 29.

Gravy, page 29: Make in a similar way to tomato sauce, cooking the onions and the oil in a bowl in the microwave, then adding the flour and microwaving for 1 minute before adding the garlic and water. After this, microwave on full power for 4 minutes, stirring once. Add the soy sauce, yeast extract and salt and pepper to taste.

Curry Sauce, page 160: Put the butter, onion, garlic, bay leaf and spices into a bowl. Cover with plastic film, pierce twice, then microwave on full power for 4 minutes. Add the tomatoes and water, re-cover and microwave for 5 minutes. Allow to stand for 5 minutes before using. If you're adding vegetables, add these with the tomatoes and microwave for 10–15 minutes, or until the vegetables are tender. Allow to stand for 5 minutes before serving.

Bread-Based Mixtures

Slices of bread can be dried out in the microwave to make breadcrumbs; spread out the slices of bread in an even layer and microwave on full power for 1–4 minutes, or until crisp. Crush with a rolling pin or in a food processor or keep in an airtight container for use as required. For buttered crumbs, as used in the *Mushroom and Tomato Layer*, spread out fresh crumbs on a large plate, dot with butter, and microwave on full power for 5 minutes, until crisp, stirring several times. Add the onion, nuts, herbs and seasoning. Assemble the dish as described, then microwave on full power for 5 minutes; allow to stand for 5 minutes before serving.

Bread Pizza, page 39: Brush the bread halves with oil, as described, then place on a large plate and microwave for 4 minutes on each side, until crisp. To finish the pizza, put on the topping as described in the recipe, then microwave on full power for 5 minutes, until heated through and the cheese melted. Allow to stand for 5 minutes, then serve.

Savoury puddings such as the *Savoury Bread and Butter Pudding*, page 35, and the *Easy Cheese Pudding* on page 36 can be baked in the microwave; microwave on full power for 3 minutes, or until puffed up and set. Stand for 5 minutes before eating. The onion and pepper for the Tomato Bread Pudding can be microwaved in a bowl with the butter (as described for soups, above) for 4 minutes before mixing with the other ingredients, then the completed pudding can be baked in a shallow dish, uncovered, on full power for 5 minutes, followed by 5 minutes standing time before serving.

Egg and Cheese Dishes

The sauce and potatoes for the *Cheese Egg Pie* can be individually cooked in the microwave, see page 46 for the sauce, and page 218 for the potatoes. Don't try to hardboil the eggs in the microwave, though. This is one thing you can't do in the microwave – they explode! Assemble the dish as described in the recipe, then microwave on full for 7–10 minutes, until heated through. Pop under a hot grill for a minute or two to brown the top, if possible.

Piperade, on page 46, is an excellent dish to make in the microwave. Put the butter into a glass or pottery mixing bowl or casserole dish and add the onion and pepper; cover with plastic film, punch a couple of times. Microwave on full for 3 minutes, or until tender, then uncover and stir in the tomatoes and garlic. Microwave on full for 1–2 minutes, then uncover again and pour in the beaten eggs and seasoning. Microwave, uncovered, on full, for about 2 minutes, or until the eggs are just set, stirring every 30 seconds. Let the mixture stand for 1 minute, then serve.

Spanish Omelette, page 47, is made in a similar way in the microwave, except that once the beaten eggs have been added you microwave the mixture, uncovered, on full, for about 4 minutes, or until the eggs are just set.

Baked Eggs, page 48, take just 2 minutes on full power for each baked egg. Let the eggs stand for 5 minutes before serving.

Soufflés cannot be made in a microwave.

Batter

Savoury Brazil Nut Fritters, page 52, are best fried rather than microwaved. *Mushroom Toad in the Hole*, page 53, can be cooked in the microwave. Use a non- metallic shallow container. Preheat the oil on high power for 1 minute, then pour in the batter and microwave for 5 minutes. Allow to stand for 5 minutes before using.

Savoury Olive Cake, page 54: Spoon the mixture into a pottery or china container. Microwave on full power for 10 minutes. Allow to stand for 10 minutes before serving; crisp under a hot grill if required.

Pasta

Pasta takes roughly the same amount of time to cook in the microwave as it does in a saucepan. The only difference is that you have a casserole dish to wash up at the end instead of a saucepan! If you want to use the microwave, put the pasta into a casserole dish with enough boiling water to cover the pasta by 1 cm (½ inch). Microwave on full until the pasta is tender: as a rough guide, this takes 7–8 minutes for 225 g (8 oz) spaghetti or tagliatelle, 6–7 minutes for 225 g (8 oz) macaroni, plus, in each case, 5 minutes standing time after cooking. If you're cooking less than 225 g (8 oz), you'll need to allow less time; look at the pasta at half time.

Sometimes it makes more sense, time-wise, to cook the pasta in a saucepan of water on top of the cooker so that you can use the microwave for making the sauce. This is true of *Tagliatelli Verde with Lentil Sauce*, page 65. To make the sauce in the microwave, put the onion and oil into a bowl and microwave for 2 minutes, then add the remaining ingredients, cover with plastic film and pierce 2–3 times, then microwave on full for 10 minutes, or until the lentils are tender, stirring two or three times. Remove from the heat and allow to stand for 5 minutes. Stir, check seasoning and serve.

For *Pasta with Green Lentils and Tomatoes*, page 67, cover the lentils with boiling water, microwave on full for 20 minutes, stand for 5 minutes. Put the onion and butter into a bowl and microwave on full power for 2 minutes, then add the cooked and drained lentils and all the other sauce ingredients and microwave on full for 5 minutes. Let the mixture stand for 5 minutes before serving.

The macaroni for *Macaroni Cheese*, page 68, and also the sauce, can be made as described above. The completed dish can be microwaved on full for about 5 minutes, but I think it is better cooked under the grill to give a nice golden brown topping.

Macaroni Bake, page 69: Cook the macaroni in the microwave as described on page 69. Put the chopped onion into a bowl with the oil, cover with plastic film, pierce two or three times, and microwave on full for 2 minutes, then add the mushrooms and tomatoes and microwave for another 2 minutes. Add the egg and microwave for 1 minute, stirring after 30 seconds. Stand for 2 minutes, then mix in the rest of the ingredients, spoon into a dish, cover with crumbs, and microwave on full for about 7 minutes, until the crumbs on top are crisp.

Pasta with Leeks and Cheese, page 70: Cook the pasta rings as described on page 61. Let them stand, covered, while you microwave the leeks: put into a wide, shallow dish, sprinkle with 4 tablespoons of water, cover with plastic film, pierce several times, then microwave on full for 4–5 minutes, or until the leeks are just tender. Let them stand while you drain the pasta and put it into a suitable shallow heatproof dish, then drain the leeks and put on top of the pasta. Sprinkle with the cheese. Microwave on full for about 5 minutes, until the cheese has melted.

Macaroni with Tomatoes, Onions and Cheese, page 70: Cook the macaroni in the microwave as described on page 216. Let the macaroni stand while you put the chopped onion into a bowl with the oil, cover with plastic film, pierce two or three times, and microwave on full for 5 minutes, then add the tomatoes and microwave for another 2 minutes. Drain the macaroni, put it into a shallow heatproof dish, pour the tomato mixture on top, sprinkle with grated cheese and grill as above, or microwave for about 5 minutes, until the cheese has melted.

Potatoes

Potatoes can be baked in a microwave, although they are not as good as conventionally-baked ones because the skins are not crisp and brown. To microwave them, just prick them, place in the oven and microwave on full power for 4–5 minutes for each potato, or until they are soft when squeezed. To boil, cut the potatoes into smallish, even-sized pieces, place in a shallow container with 1cm (½ inch) water. Cover and microwave on high for 12–16 minutes or until tender.

Potato and Cheese Layer, page 77: Prepare as described, using a microwave-proof shallow casserole dish. Cover with plastic film, pierce several times, then microwave on full for 15–20 minutes, until the potatoes in the centre of the dish are tender. Let the dish stand for 5–10 minutes before serving: reheat for 2 minutes if necessary.

Potato Hotpot, page 80: Bake in the microwave on full power for 10 minutes, plus 10 minutes standing.

The individual components for the *Potato and Mushroom Gratin*, page 82 – the potatoes, and the mushroom sauce – can be cooked in the microwave as described above, then the assembled dish can be microwaved on full power, uncovered, for 5–10 minutes, until heated through.

Vegetables

Vegetables cook well in a microwave, requiring the minimum of water and retaining their full colour. Prepare the vegetables as usual and cut into even-sized pieces, not too big. Put these into a shallow, wide microwave-proof dish, if possible, so that they are spread out. Sprinkle 2–4 tablespoons of water on top, cover with plastic film, pierce several times for the steam to escape. Then microwave on full until the vegetables are tender, stirring once or twice. After cooking, let the vegetables stand, still covered, for 5–10 minutes, to continue cooking in their own heat. The timing of the vegetables depends on the size of the pieces, the type of vegetable, and the quantity being cooked, but as a general rule, potatoes or root vegetables take 20 minutes for a 4-servings quantity, about 5 minutes for a single serving; cabbage and spinach take about 6 minutes for 4 servings, 3–4 minutes for 1 serving.

Vegetable dishes, such as the *Cabbage and Cashew Nut Stir-Fry* on page 86, can be cooked in a shallow container in the microwave. Put the cabbage with the oil and turmeric into a shallow container, cover with plastic film, pierce several times. Microwave on full for 2–3 minutes, stirring a couple of times, then add the rest of the ingredients, stir well, re-cover and microwave for a further 2–3 minutes, until the cabbage is the right tenderness for you. Let the mixture stand for a few minutes before serving.

Sweet and Sour Cabbage and Peanut Stir-Fry, page 87: Make this in the same way as *Cabbage and Cashew Nut Stir-Fry*, but start by putting the peanuts and oil into a shallow container, cover with plastic film, pierce several times. Microwave on full for 2–3 minutes, stirring a couple of times, then add the rest of the vegetables, stir well, re-cover and microwave for a further 2–3 minutes. Add the sweet and sour mixture, re-cover, microwave for 2–3 minutes. Let the mixture stand for a few minutes before serving.

Ratatouille, page 88: Put the onions, pepper and oil into a large shallow microwave-proof dish, cover with plastic film, pierce several times. Microwave on full power for 4 minutes, stirring once or twice, then put in the crushed garlic, courgettes, aubergine and tomatoes, re- cover and microwave on full power for 7–10 minutes, until the vegetables are tender. Let the mixture stand, covered, for 10 minutes. Season, sprinkle with parsley and serve.

Cheese and Aubergine Bake, page 89: Put the onion, salted and rinsed aubergine, and the oil, into a shallow microwave-proof dish, cover with plastic film, pierce several times. Microwave on full power for 4–5 minutes, until the vegetables are tender, stirring three times. Then layer the aubergines and onions with the tomatoes and cheeses, as above. Microwave for 10–15 minutes, until cooked through in the centre.

Root Vegetable Crumble, page 90: Layer the vegetables into a microwave-proof dish. Microwave, uncovered, on full power for 8 minutes. Allow to stand for 5 minutes before serving.

Sweetcorn Bake, page 91: First put the butter and milk into a bowl, microwave on full power for 1–2 minutes, until the butter has melted, then add the bread and complete the recipe as described above. Microwave the completed dish, covered, on full power for 8 minutes. Allow to stand for 10 minutes before using.

Stuffed Peppers, page 102: Put the peppers into a deep casserole dish or bowl, cover with plastic film, pierce the plastic film a few times, and microwave for 5 minutes, turning the peppers 'sides to middle' half way through. Put the chopped onion into a bowl with the oil, cover with plastic film, pierce two or three times, and microwave on full for 2 minutes, then add the mushrooms and microwave for another 2 minutes. Add the nuts and flavourings, then pack the mixture into the peppers. Put the peppers into a casserole dish, cover with plastic film, pierce several times, and microwave for 6–8 minutes, until the peppers are cooked through. Stand for 4–5 minutes before serving.

Stuffed Avocado, page 103: Put the onion, pepper and butter into a bowl, cover with plastic film, pierce several times, then microwave on full power for 4 minutes. Stir in the rest of the stuffing ingredients, then pile this mixture into the avocado halves. Put the avocado halves into a suitable flat dish, microwave on full power for 2–3 minutes, until just heated through. Serve at once.

Stuffed Aubergines, page 104: Brush the aubergine skins on both sides with a little oil; lay the skins on a flat dish and microwave, uncovered, for 1 minute on each side. Put the aubergine flesh, onion, tomato and garlic into a bowl with a tablespoonful of oil, cover with plastic film, pierce a few times, then microwave for 4–5 minutes, until tender, stirring twice. Add the rest of the stuffing ingredients, spoon the mixture into the aubergine skins, sprinkle with crumbs, and microwave for 6 minutes, until heated through and crisp on top.

Stuffed Cabbage Rolls, page 105: Spread the cabbage leaves out on a shallow microwave-proof dish, sprinkle a few drops of water over each, cover with plastic film, pierce a few times, and microwave for 2–3 minutes, until the leaves have softened. Let them stand for 2–3 minutes. Put the onion into a bowl with the oil, cover with plastic film, pierce a few times, and microwave for 4 minutes, until tender, then add the rest of the ingredients. Fill the leaves with stuffing, place in a dish and cover with sauce, as described above, then microwave for about 5 minutes, until cooked through, and stand for 4–5 minutes before serving.

Tomatoes with Spicy Stuffing, page 106: Prepare the tomatoes as described in the recipe. To make the filling, put the onion, potato, oil and spices into a bowl, cover with plastic film, pierce a few times, then microwave on full power for 4 minutes, stirring once. Season, then spoon this mixture into the tomatoes. Put the tomatoes into a suitable container, together with the scooped-out pulp, and microwave on full power for 4 minutes. Let them stand for 4 minutes, then serve.

The filling for *Tomatoes with Courgette and Corn Stuffing*, page 107, can also be prepared in the microwave. Put the onion and butter into a bowl, cover with plastic film, pierce a few times, then microwave on full power for 2 minutes, stirring once, then add the garlic, courgette and sweetcorn, re-cover and microwave for a further 2 minutes. Season, then spoon this mixture into the tomatoes. Put the tomatoes into a suitable container, together with the scooped-out pulp, and microwave on full power for 4 minutes. Let them stand for 4 minutes, then serve.

Marrow with Sage and Onion Stuffing, page 108: Put the onion and butter into a bowl, cover with plastic film, pierce several times, then microwave on full for 4 minutes. Add the rest of the stuffing ingredients. Fill the marrow with stuffing as described and place in a lightly-greased dish. Cover with plastic film, pierce several times, and microwave until the marrow is tender in the centre. The time will vary according to the size of the marrow, but allow 5 minutes for a large courgette, 10 minutes for a small marrow, and 15–20 minutes for a larger marrow.

Pastry Dishes

Quick Quiche, page 110: Prepare as described in the recipe, using a non-metal flan dish or dishes. Microwave on full for 6 minutes for a large flan or 2 small ones, 3 minutes for 1 small flan. Allow to stand for 5 minutes before serving.

Poverty Pie, page 113: Use a non-metallic flan dish; microwave the flan case, covered, on full power for 6 minutes. Put the butter into a bowl and microwave for 1–2 minutes, until melted, then add the flour and microwave for 1 minute. Stir in the milk and microwave for 1–2 minutes, until thickened. Add the rest of the ingredients as described above, pour into the flan case. Microwave, uncovered, on full power for 8 minutes. Leave to stand for 5 minutes before using.

Mixed Vegetable Flan, page 113: Microwave the flan case (in a non-metallic dish), uncovered, on full power for 6 minutes. Put the frozen vegetables and cauliflower florets into a shallow dish, cover with plastic film, pierce two or three times, then microwave on full for 6–8 minutes, stirring twice, or until the vegetables are just tender. Mix the vegetables with the sauce and put into the flan case as described above, then microwave, uncovered, on full power for 8 minutes. Leave to stand for 5 minutes before using. Pop the flan under a hot grill for a minute or two to brown the top if you wish, or decorate with some slices of tomato.

Mushroom Flan, page 115: Put the pastry into a non-metallic flan dish; microwave, uncovered, on full power for 6 minutes. Put the onion and butter into a bowl, cover with plastic film, pierce two or three times and microwave on full for 2 minutes, then add the mushrooms and microwave for 2–3 minutes, or until the mushrooms are just tender, stirring once. Stir in the cornflour, microwave for 1 minute, then stir in the soured cream and microwave for 1 minute. Add seasoning, spread the mixture into the flan. Microwave, uncovered, for 5 minutes, then leave to stand for 5 minutes.

Cheese and Onion Pie, page 117: Put the onion into a bowl, sprinkle with 4 tablespoons water, cover with clingfilm, pierce three times. Microwave on full for 4–5 minutes, until the onions are tender, stirring twice. Leave, uncovered, until cold. Assemble the pie as described above. Microwave on full power for 10 minutes. Allow to stand for 10 minutes before serving.

Potato and Mushroom Pasties, page 119: Put the onions into a large bowl with the oil, cover with plastic film, pierce twice and microwave on full power for 2 minutes, stirring once. Then add the potatoes, and microwave on full power for a further 2 minutes, stirring once. Put in the mushrooms, microwave on full power for 1–2 minutes, until all the vegetables are tender, stirring once. Cool. Roll out the pastry and assemble the pasties as described in the recipe, then microwave them for 8–10 minutes. Allow the pasties to stand for 5 minutes before eating.

Vegetable Pudding, page 120: Prepare as described in the recipe, using a microwave-proof bowl. Cover the pudding with greaseproof paper or a roasting bag, tie with string. Stand the pudding in a deep non-metallic container and pour boiling water around it. Microwave on full power for 30 minutes for a big pudding, 20 minutes for a two-person size and 15 minutes for a one-person size. Let the pudding stand, undisturbed, for 10 minutes before serving.

Quick Pizza, page 122: Put the base on to a non-metallic plate and microwave on full power for 3 minutes. For the topping, put the onions and oil into a large bowl, cover with plastic film, pierce two or three times and microwave on full power for 4 minutes, until tender, stirring twice. Add the rest of the ingredients, spread on top of the pizza base. Microwave for 8–10 minutes.

Nut Dishes

Most basic savoury nut mixtures begin with frying an onion in butter or oil, and this can be done in the microwave by putting these ingredients into a bowl, covering with plastic film, pierced two or three times, and microwaving on full for 4 minutes. After this, if flour has to be added, to make a sauce-base, mix in the flour, return to the oven and microwave for 1 minute, then stir in the water. Return to the oven and microwave on full for 1–2 minutes, until thickened. Remove from the oven and stir in the rest of the ingredients. Form into burgers and fry, or put into a greased casserole and microwave on full power for 8–10 minutes, until firm in the centre. Let the roast stand for 5 minutes, then serve. The *Quick Savoury Nut Roast*, page 127, only takes about 5 minutes to bake, followed by 5 minutes standing time.

Chestnut Casserole, page 130: Put the onion and celery into a bowl with the butter, cover with plastic film, pierce two or three times, and microwave on full for 4 minutes, stirring once. Then add the rest of the ingredients, stir well, and microwave on full for 10 minutes, or until the vegetables are tender, stirring once or twice. Stand for 5 minutes before serving.

Lentils

Split orange lentils cook quickly and cleanly in the microwave. Put the lentils into a bowl with the water, cover with plastic film, pierce twice, then microwave on full power for 10 minutes, stirring 3 times, then leave them to stand, covered, for 5 minutes.

Green lentils also microwave well. Put the lentils and water into a deep bowl, cover with plastic film, pierce two or three times, microwave on full power for 20 minutes, or until tender, stirring two or three times, then let them stand, covered, for 5 minutes.

The split orange lentils can be used to make *Lentil Roast*, p 000, but I think this is best baked in a shallow dish and sprinkled with buttered crumbs if it is going to be baked in the microwave. It should be cooked on full power for 8–10 minutes, followed by 5 minutes standing. The lentils and vegetable mixture for *Spicy Lentil Burgers*, page 134, can be cooked in the microwave, too, but I think these are best finished off by frying as usual.

Lentil Dal, page 135, is excellent made in the microwave: put the onion and butter into a bowl, cover with plastic film, pierce two or three times, then microwave on full power for 4 minutes, stirring twice. Add the lentils and the rest of the ingredients, cover with plastic film, pierce a couple of times and microwave on full power for 10 minutes, stirring two or three times, until the lentils are tender. Leave to stand, covered, for 5 minutes. If you are making a smaller quantity, for one or two people, the microwaving times will be less: 2 minutes for the onion, and for the whole mixture, 3–5 minutes, plus standing time.

Lentils and Mushrooms au Gratin, page 136: Put the lentils and milk-and-water into a deep bowl, cover with plastic film, pierce a couple of times and microwave on full power for 10 minutes, stirring two or three times, until the lentils are tender. Leave to stand, covered, for 5 minutes. If you are making a smaller quantity, for one or two people, the microwaving times will be less: 2 minutes for the onion, and for the whole mixture, 3–5 minutes, plus standing time. While the lentils are standing, put the onion and butter into a bowl, cover with plastic film, pierce two or three times, then microwave on full power for 4 minutes, stirring twice. Put the mushrooms and butter into the base of a casserole that's large enough to take the complete mixture, cover with plastic film and microwave on full power for 2 minutes. Complete the lentil mixture as described in the recipe, pour it over the mushrooms, sprinkle with crumbs and cheese, then microwave on full power, uncovered, for 6–8 minutes. Allow to stand for 5 minutes before serving.

Green lentils, cooked in the microwave, can be made into *Lentils with Tomatoes and Thyme*, page 137, the onion can either be fried in the microwave, as described above, or in a pan in the usual way. After mixing this, and the rest of the ingredients, with the cooked lentils, season to taste, and microwave for about 3 minutes, just to heat through.

Lentil Shepherd's Pie, page 137: Cook the lentils as described above. Put the onion and butter into a bowl, cover with plastic film, pierce two or three times, then microwave on full power for 4 minutes, stirring once. Add the rest of the ingredients and the drained lentils, season and put into a shallow dish. To make the potato topping, put the potatoes into a large bowl with 4 tablespoons of milk and a knob of butter. Cover with plastic film, pierce two or three times, microwave on full power for 6–8 minutes, or until the potatoes are tender. Season and mash, adding a little more milk if necessary. Spread this on top of the lentils. Microwave, uncovered, on full power, for 5 minutes, stand for 5 minutes. Pop under the grill for a minute or two to brown the top if required.

Dried Beans

To do the hot quick soak, put the beans into a bowl with water to cover generously. Cover with plastic film, pierce twice. Microwave on full power until the water comes to the boil, then continue to microwave for 1 minute. Allow the beans to stand, covered, for 1 hour.

To cook soaked beans, put them into a bowl with enough water to cover them, cover with plastic film, pierce two or three times, then microwave on full until tender: 45 minutes for 225 g (8 oz) red kidney beans and bean mix, followed by 15 minutes standing time, covered; 25 minutes on full for 225 g (8 oz) chick peas, plus 10 minutes standing time; 10 minutes for 225 g (8 oz) split peas, plus 10 minutes standing time.

Middle Eastern Chick Pea Stew, page 144: Put the onion into a bowl with 2 tablespoons oil, cover with plastic film, pierce twice, then microwave on full power for 2 minutes. Add the aubergine pieces, stir, then cover again and microwave on full power for 2–4 minutes, until the aubergine is tender, stirring twice. Add the rest of the ingredients, cover and microwave on full power for 4 minutes. Stand for 5–10 minutes before serving.

Easy Vegetable and Red Kidney Bean Stew, page 146: Put the onion into a large bowl with the oil, pepper, carrots, leeks or courgettes or celery. Cover with plastic film, pierce two or three times, then microwave on full power for 4 minutes, stirring twice. Add the rest of the ingredients, cover as before, and microwave on full power for 5 minutes. Allow to stand for 5 minutes before serving.

Pease Pudding, page 151: Prepare the split peas as described above. While the peas are standing, put the onion and butter into a bowl, cover with plastic film, pierce two or three times, then microwave on full power for 4 minutes, stirring twice. Mix all the ingredients together and spoon into a suitable shallow dish as described above. Microwave for 6 minutes. Stand for 5–10 minutes before serving.

Grains

Rice, page 156: Put the rice into a microwave-proof container with water and a little salt, using the proportions of 1 cup of rice to 2 cups of water. Cover with plastic film, pierce twice. Microwave on full power, without stirring, for 25 minutes. Leave to stand, still covered, for 10 minutes, then fluff with a fork and use.

Spiced Rice, page 159: First put the onion and oil into a bowl, stir, cover with plastic film, pierce twice, and microwave on full power for 4 minutes. Then add the rice, spices, water and salt. Re-cover and microwave on full power for 25 minutes. Then allow the rice to stand, still covered, for 10 minutes. Fluff with a fork and serve.

Rice and Courgette Gratin, page 157: Cook the rice as described above. Put the onion, courgettes and oil into a bowl, cover with plastic film, pierce two or three times, then microwave on full power for 5–6 minutes, stirring twice. Add the rest of the ingredients, as described above, spoon the mixture into a shallow microwave-proof dish, sprinkle with grated cheese and microwave on full power, uncovered, for 6 minutes. Allow to stand for 5 minutes. Finish this off under a hot grill for a minute or two if you want a brown topping.

Vegetable Rice with Roasted Nuts, page 157: Put the onion and oil into a bowl, cover with plastic film, pierce two or three times, then microwave on full power for 2 minutes, stirring once. Add the turmeric, rice, garlic and water. Stir, then cover with plastic film, pierce twice and microwave for 10 minutes. Then put the carrot, pepper, beans or leeks onto the bowl on top of the rice, without stirring. Re-cover and microwave for 5 minutes. Then add the tomatoes, cover again, and microwave for a further 5 minutes. Add the nuts, re-cover, and allow to stand for 10 minutes. Fork up gently, check seasoning, and serve.

Quick Oat Savoury, page 162: Layer the ingredients into a shallow microwave-proof container. Microwave on full power for 5 minutes; allow to stand for 5 minutes before serving.

Barley Casserole, page 164: Put the onion and oil into a bowl, cover with plastic film, pierce two or three times, then microwave on full power for 2 minutes, stirring twice. Add the rest of the ingredients, stir, re-cover, and microwave on full power for 2 minutes. Then add the barley, water and stock powder. Re-cover, then microwave on full power for 10 minutes. Add the mushrooms, microwave for 2 minutes. Allow to stand for 10 minutes. Check seasoning, sprinkle with chopped parsley and serve.

Spicy Millet Pilaf, page 165: Put the millet into a bowl without any water and microwave on full power for 2–3 minutes, until it begins to smell roasted. In another bowl put the onion, carrot, garlic, ginger, cinnamon and oil, cover with plastic film, pierce twice and microwave on full power for 2 minutes. Add the millet, water and salt. Cover with plastic film, pierce twice, then microwave on full power for 15 minutes. Leave to stand for 10 minutes. Add the nuts and raisins, check seasoning and serve.

Bulgur Pilaf, page 166: Put the onion into a bowl with the red pepper and oil, cover with plastic film, pierce two or three times, then microwave on full power for 3 minutes, stirring twice. Add the garlic, ginger and cinnamon, re-cover and microwave on full for 1 minute. Add the bulgur wheat, water and some seasoning. Cover with plastic film, pierce twice and microwave on full power for 10 minutes. Allow to stand for 10 minutes. Fluff with a fork and add the nuts and raisins.

Bulgur Pilaf with Red Lentils, page 167: Put the onion into a bowl with the oil, cover with plastic film, pierce two or three times, then microwave on full power for 3 minutes, stirring twice. Add the garlic and ginger, re-cover and microwave on full for 1 minute. Add the bulgur wheat, lentils, water and some seasoning. Cover with plastic film, pierce twice and microwave on full power for 15 minutes. Allow to stand for 10 minutes. Fluff with a fork and add the parsley and lemon juice, and seasoning to taste.

Buckwheat Bake, page 168: Put the onion, carrots and oil into a bowl, cover with plastic film, pierce two or three times, then microwave on full power for 3 minutes, stirring twice. Add the mushrooms and garlic, stir, re-cover and microwave on full power for 1 minute. Then put in the buckwheat, herbs, water, salt and pepper, re-cover, and microwave on full power for 15 minutes. Leave to stand for 10 minutes. Stir in the soy sauce and parsley, check the seasoning and serve.

Couscous with Spicy Chick Pea Stew, page 169: Put the onion into a bowl with the carrot and oil, cover with plastic film, pierce two or three times, then microwave on full power for 4 minutes, stirring twice. Stir in the spices, re-cover and microwave for 1 minute. Then add the raisins, chick peas (or broad beans, peas or sweetcorn), water and tomato puree. Re-cover, microwave on full power for 10–15 minutes, until everything is cooked through. Leave to stand while you put the soaked couscous into a greased bowl, cover with plastic film, pierce twice, and microwave for 5 minutes, stirring once. Leave to stand for 5 minutes, then serve with the stew.

Gnocchi, page 171: Put the milk into a large bowl and microwave on full power for 1–2 minutes, until boiling. Then sprinkle the semolina on top, whisking until smooth. Add the seasoning, then microwave, uncovered, for about 5 minutes, until thickened, stirring at the end of every minute to keep the sauce smooth. Remove from the oven and continue as above. The assembled dish is best grilled rather than microwaved, though you could microwave for 6 minutes.

Cheese Fritters, page 172: Put the milk into a large bowl with the bay leaf, onion and clove and microwave on full power for 1–2 minutes, until boiling. Cover and leave to stand for 15 minutes, then remove the bay leaf, onion and clove. Put the milk back into the oven and microwave for about 1 minute, to bring back to the boil. Then sprinkle the semolina on top, whisking until smooth. Add the seasoning, then microwave, uncovered, for about 5 minutes, until thickened, stirring at the end of every minute to keep the sauce smooth. Remove from the oven, add the cheese and continue as above. Shallow-fry the fritters as described.

Puddings

Baked Apples, page 177: Prepare the apples as described in the recipe, put into a suitable dish, cover with plastic film, pierced twice to let out the steam. Microwave on full power allowing 1½ minutes for each apple. Let the apples stand, still covered, for 5–6 minutes before serving.

Stewed Apples, page 177: Put the apples, butter and water into a bowl, cover with plastic film, pierce a couple of times and microwave on full power for 8 minutes (allow 2 minutes for each 225 g (8 oz) of fruit). Leave to stand for 4–5 minutes, then stir in the sugar.

Stewed Rhubarb, Gooseberries, Blackberries, Blackcurrants, Plums, page 178: microwave as for stewed apples.

Fruit Meringue: I do not think this is as good cooked in the microwave. Prepare the dish as described, then microwave on full power for 4 minutes. This will set the meringue, but it will not be crisp. Brown off the top under the grill if you wish.

Veiled Country Lass, page 181: The crumb part of this cooks beautifully in a microwave. Put the crumbs, butter and sugar into a large bowl and microwave on full power, uncovered, for about 5 minutes, stirring every minute or so, until the crumbs are crisp and beginning to brown.

Apple Charlotte, page 181: Put the crumbs, butter and sugar into a large bowl and microwave on full power, uncovered, for about 5 minutes, stirring every minute or so, until the crumbs are crisp and beginning to brown.

Bread and Butter Pudding, page 184: Prepare pudding as described. Microwave, uncovered, on full power for 4–5 minutes, until set. Allow to stand for 5 minutes before using.

Steamed Pudding, page 184: Cover the pudding with plastic film. Microwave on full power for 4 minutes (2–3 minutes for smaller ones). Stand for 5 minutes before serving.

Fruit Sponge Pudding, page 185: Microwave uncovered, on full power, for 5 minutes for a 4-person size, 2–3 minutes for smaller puddings, or until the sponge springs back in the centre and at the sides. Allow to stand for 5 minutes.

Fruit Crumble, page 186: Microwave the crumble, uncovered, for 10 minutes (3–5 minutes for one or two person size crumbles). Allow to stand for 5 minutes. Brown under a hot grill to crisp and colour the top.

Strawberry Tart, page 187: Use a non-metallic flan dish. Microwave the pastry on full power, uncovered, for 6 minutes, or until set and firm. Melt the jam in a small bowl on full power for about 2 minutes.

Treacle Tart, page 189: Melt the syrup in a small bowl in the microwave on full power for about 2 minutes, or until liquid. Use a non-metallic dish for the flan; microwave on full power for 10 minutes; allow to stand for 10 minutes before serving.

Top Crust Apple Pie, page 189: Microwave the pie on full power for 10 minutes (about 4 minutes for a smaller one); allow to stand for 5–10 minutes before serving.

Double Crust Fruit Pie, page 191: Microwave on full power for about 8 minutes (3–4 for a smaller pie) until the top is 'set'; allow to stand for 5 minutes. Sprinkle with demerara sugar before serving.

Oven-Baked Egg Custard, page 193: Microwave, uncovered, on full power, for 4–5 minutes, until set.

Cooker-Top Egg Custard, page 194: Blend the cornflour and eggs with a little milk in a small bowl as described. Put the rest of the milk into a large bowl and bring to the boil in the microwave — takes about 2 minutes on full power. Pour some of this milk onto the cornflour mixture, then tip it back into the big bowl. Microwave, uncovered, on full power, for 4–5 minutes, stirring at the end of every minute.

Bread and Cakes

Easy Wholewheat Scones, page 199: Microwave on full power, uncovered, for 4 minutes. Allow to stand for 5 minutes before cooling on a wire rack.

Cheese Scones, page 199: As for plain scones, above.

Wholewheat Jam Tarts, page 200: Microwave on full power for 4 minutes. Allow to stand for 5 minutes.

Date Fingers, page 201: Microwave on full power for 5 minutes; allow to stand for 5 minutes.

Quick and Easy Fruit Cake, page 202: Microwave on full power for 10 minutes, then on defrost for 10 minutes. Allow to stand for 10 minutes.

Rock Cakes, page 203: Microwave on full power for 5 minutes. Allow the cakes to stand for 5 minutes.

Flapjacks, page 204: Put the butter and sugar into a bowl and microwave, uncovered, for 2–3 minutes, until melted. Add the rest of the ingredients, press into a suitable shallow dish. Microwave for 5 minutes. Allow to cool in the dish.

Parkin, page 204: Put the sugar, treacle, golden syrup and butter into a large bowl and microwave on full power for 2–3 minutes until melted. Cool slightly, then add the rest of the ingredients and pour the mixture into a suitable shallow non-metal container. Microwave on full power for 10 minutes, then on defrost for 10 minutes. Allow to cool in the tin.

Gingerbread, page 205: Put the honey, treacle, sugar and butter into a large bowl and microwave on full power for 2–3 minutes, until melted. Cool, then add the rest of the ingredients. Pour the mixture into a suitable dish. Microwave on full power for 10 minutes, then on defrost for 10 minutes. Cool in the tin.

All-in-one Sponge, page 206: Use one deep 20 cm (8 inch) microwave baking container or soufflé dish. Line with greaseproof paper. Fill with the mixture, level the top. Microwave on full power for 5 minutes. Allow to stand for 5 minutes, then remove from the container and cool on a wire rack.

Iced Fingers, page 207: Use a special microwave cake dish or suitable shallow casserole dish. Microwave for 5 minutes. Allow to stand for 5 minutes.

Quick Buns, page 209: Use a special microwave bun tin or paper cake cases standing on a microwave-proof tray. Microwave for 5 minutes. Allow to stand for 5 minutes.

Shortbread, page 209: Microwave the round shortbread (in a suitable container) on full power for 5 minutes, then let it cool in the container. Microwave the biscuits for 6 minutes; allow them to stand for 5 minutes, then cool on a wire rack.

Wholemeal Bread, page 210: Use glass, pottery or plastic moulds to bake the bread in. Bake the loaves, uncovered, on full power for 5 minutes. Allow to stand for 5 minutes before turning out onto a cooling rack.

Index